SWIMMING UPSTREAM

by
Christine Roush

Jenna,

Hope you do a better job of listening to what I write than watching what I manage to do 😊 Focus on what matters in life — family, friends & the things God cares about — people.

I love you!

First published by Dog Ear Publishing
4010 W. 86th Street, Ste H
Indianapolis, IN 46268
www.dogearpublishing.net

ISBN: 978-160844-020-7

This book is printed on acid-free paper.

Printed in the United States of America

Table of Contents

Swimming Upstream
Reflections on Consumerism and Culture

Acknowledgements

This book has only been possible because of all the shoulders upon which I have stood, and I have many to thank. People matter a great deal to me, and none more than my family. I was blessed by great parents, Keith and Beulah Burch. They laid a firm foundation, and have watched with fear and trepidation to see if it would withstand the storms. So far so good Mom and Dad. My husband David walks this path with me every day, and I could ask for no better partner in the journey. He is my best friend, the sunshine in my life, and the one who keeps me sane. Dave and my daughters Kirsten, Megan and "adopted daughter" Jenna make life worth the effort – thank-you and I love you all.

My early role models, Pastors S. Benjamin Hamblett III, my Uncle, Jack Wolfe, and Jose Ortiz, all challenged me to listen for the call of the Lord in my life and led by example. Colleagues and mentors Howard Washburn and Bill Carlsen called me to my better self in my early years and forgave my lack of life experience, and Ron Vallet fanned a flame for stewardship education. He has forgotten more than I will ever learn. I owe them all much. To First Baptist Endicott, the first to invest and encourage me in the topic of stewardship resource development – all God's best! May the seeds we planted bear fruit.

Wayne Brown and the American Baptist Churches Oregon gave me the freedom to continue my education while pursuing ministry, and encouraged me in the learning process; and Bob Crandall made sure I could keep the mortgage paid and my head above water. You invested much in this project and in me Bob – thank-you. You are truly the best!

George Fox Seminary worked hard to broaden my worldview, and stretched me a great deal in the process. All my thanks and appreciation go out to Dan Brunner who suffered through a whole series of papers and a final dissertation in the quest to make me a better writer and teach me to be a kinder, gentler child of God. It was an honor and a privilege to be guided through my journey by both Dan and Len Sweet. Len's probing questions and rare "bingo's" challenged me beyond my comfort level and my traditions into the world of the *Perfect Storm*. Thank you Dan and Len. To Debbie Herr who slogged through the proofing of countless papers and manuscripts—I am in your debt. To Pat and Jean for providing a quiet spot to write—thanks for being a part of my extended family.

To my fellow travelers in *Church in the Emerging Culture* D. Min. module 5—Brian Ross, Bryan Benjamin, Denis Bell, Fourie van den Berg, Greg Glatz, Henry Berg, Jake Youmans, Jeff Tacklind, John Frank, Kerry McRoberts, Lars Rood, Patrick Murunga, Quintin Moore, Randy Groves and Chuck Coward—thank you for allowing me into your lives and for sharing insights into your ministries with me on a weekly basis. You have done much to shape my thinking, and I miss our chats.

To Jeff Savage and my church family at First Baptist Springfield, and to First Baptist South New Berlin my first church home, thank you for surrounding me with a family & a community of faith. God is good, all the time.

Special Thanks to those who contributed stories and ideas of Swimming Upstream

Barbara Galbraith
Jennifer Sanborn
Lisa Roush
Brenda Burkholder
Al Wright

Introduction

A few words to start with.

It seems only fair to tell you upfront, I am a plain Jane thinker. If it is deep spiritual truth and astounding scriptural exegesis you are after – you want a different book.

An English teacher friend once shared that he told a particularly annoying group of 10th graders that they were idiots. Since he used words none of them had heard before, he was confident they were clueless about the insult. While clearly a nifty tool when talking with your crazy neighbor or detested colleague at work – big words will not be a trick I employ. Instead, I have strong feelings about the culture where we live, and I want to share them with you. I want everyone to easily understand because I believe we are fast approaching a time when it will be too late.

There will be no convoluted reasoning, no deep arguments based on obscure interpretation. Instead, I want to work with the facts. Clearly they will be my version of facts. My goal is for you to wrestle with them and decide for yourself. These facts include that God gave us a system for living our lives. We turned a deaf ear to that plan. That mistake brought tragic consequences for many of us personally—and certainly for God's creation as a whole.

This book is about the last hundred years. We gave up something important, but failed to realize the importance until it was too late. We traveled from being the masters of our own destiny to slaves of our own choices.

I had a great T-Shirt once. In fact, I wore it so much and it had so many holes that my family would not let me out of the house while wearing it. It said

Any old fish can tumble down the stream. Go against the flow.

We stopped going against the flow. You and me and our kids. Now we are travelling downstream with the flow just like everybody else. As much as we Americans want to see ourselves as independent spirits and rugged individualist types like John Wayne, we are not. Many of us look and act pretty much alike. How did that happen?

My religion means a lot to me. How did I start looking like everybody else? How did I become a card carrying member of a culture bent on consuming everything in sight, with the credit card debt to prove it? I am a go against the flow kind of person. What happened to me?

I decided to find out. This book is about what I discovered along the way. Ultimately, it is about choosing to swim upstream.

The Happiest Fish in the Sea
The myth of more

There are two tragedies in life. One is not getting what you want. The other is getting it.

Oscar Wilde

You can't always get what you want,
You can't always get what you want.
But if you try sometimes, well you might just find,
You get what you need.

The Rolling Stones

I am not complaining about having too little. I have learned to be satisfied with whatever I have. I know what it is to be poor or to have plenty, and I have lived under all kinds of conditions. I know what it means to be full or to be hungry, to have too much or too little. Christ gives me the strength to face anything.

The Apostle Paul
Philippians 4: 11-13

Who is rich? He that is content. Who is that? Nobody.

Benjamin Franklin

"Mommy you make me happy." I still get a little misty eyed when I remember that moment when my three year old daughter spontaneously uttered those words. I never heard them from her before and have not since.

Happiness. That beast so illusive for some and always just a smile away for others. I know some folks that literally brighten a room when they enter it. I also know a few that brighten it more by leaving. What makes us happy? And are we investing our time in the things that matter to us? For myself, I was somewhat dismayed to discover my answers to those questions.

Years ago, I served as the Director of a children's camp in upstate New York. As the season came to an end, the 24 foot camp sailboat needed to be taken down the lake for winter storage at the local boatyard. Though not a task that usually fell to me, most of my staff had gone home already. So one early September afternoon, two of the remaining staff and I were half way out on the lake and sailing south. While I love to sail, the camp twelve-foot Sunfish sailboats were more my style. I would catch some wind, tip the boat as close to the water as I could, and fly across the choppy surface. Often as not, I would lean too far and flip. That's what I liked about a Sunfish. Find the centerboard and stand on it. Grab the mast and I was back in business—wet, but in business.

This boat was different. At 24 feet and a sleeper cabin underneath, one could not stand on the centerboard and right the thing anytime soon. I treated this boat with a bit more respect. Fear is the more appropriate word.

It had been a long summer. They always are in camping ministry: homesick kids and immature counselors; young staff more concerned with impressing the opposite sex than creating any truly edible food or repairing anything on the maintenance list; broken toilets and leaking roofs; and the perpetual red ink that seems to go hand in hand with ministry. As soon as this boat got where it had to go, it would finally be over for one more year.

Some of God's most beautiful work has always shown itself in lakes. The water was like glass. Though not boding well for a quick trip, it made for a spectacular image of the hills that surrounded the lake dancing on the surface of the water. This was a particularly beautiful fall day, one that reminded me why I loved camping ministry.

The long summer fell away. All the miffed parents and three hour trips to the emergency room, all the burnt hot chocolate and plugged leach fields, all of it drained from my body. My soul rejoiced. The gentle breeze and warm sun combined with the beauty which encircled me and brought a rare depth of peace to my spirit. I remembered that my world was blessed by a healthy family, a great marriage to a man I loved, and my young daughters would greet me with joy when I returned home. Every piece felt right in my world. In that moment I realized I was deeply, truly, happy.

These moments are rare in life. They are quick glimpses of what will someday come, when the Lord calls us home, moments when the cares of day to day living fall away, and the earth sings within us.

So why, if I know that time with my family and beautiful lakes bring me the greatest happiness, do I find myself spending so little meaningful time with either?

That is the part that dismays me.

I decided to think about it. Thinking about it dismayed me even more.

I do not like the answers. You may not like them either. As much as I want to believe it is the rest of the world that is materialistic and enmeshed in the larger culture, I find I am stuck too. I spend a lot of my day doing what I do not like, for the wrong reasons. So, in spite of knowing what brings me happiness I find I am not happy.

God says put your faith in me (Matthew 22:34-40). Focus on me and the things I tell you to focus on. Christ says the greatest commandment is to love God and the second greatest is to love one another (Matthew 22:36-39). Scripture tells me one of God's richest blessings to me is my family (Psalm 127:4,5). And yet one of the things I seem to find the least time for is nurturing relationships. Relationships with my spouse, my kids, my parents who are now in their retirement years, my friends and my neighbors – all the relationships that matter – find little space in my hectic life. Email and my computer I have time for. People who I actually care about—not so much.

How did my priorities get so far out of whack from what really matters to me and to God?

Psychologist Robert Frank asks, "If we would be happier and healthier working shorter hours and spending more time with our families, even though that would mean living in smaller houses and buying less expensive cars, why don't we just do it?"[1] Wow! What a great question! The answer is hard to swallow. Most of us respond with *you go first,* and *I will if you will.* A few strong and noble types have latched on to downsizing and simplifying their lives but most of us find it a very hard step to take.

Mr. Frank goes on to answer his own question with the word *context.* For instance, when I served on a mission team to build a home in Tijuana and used a pickaxe and shovel to dig in 95-degree heat all day, the shower at the church where we stayed looked like heaven. That same shower - with the large spider hidden in the back corner, dank, dirty, cracked concrete floor, and old shower curtain – would never be considered heaven in my church in Oregon. Likewise, the beat up old Chevy van we used to travel around the sprawling city of Tijuana would raise a fair number of eyebrows when parked in front of my house in my neighborhood. Our ability to downsize and simplify is deeply connected to context. What fits right in when located in one place, becomes sub-par in others.

Why is that? Why do we let others set the standards we are willing to live by? We are rugged individualists remember! We tamed the west and pulled ourselves up by our bootstraps. We are the masters of our own lives. So why give other people control over what we buy, how we dress, and what car we drive? Most of us would probably say *because that is what we like too. That is what makes us happy. Those standards are our standards, and that is how we like to live.*

The truth may surprise you. At least it did me.

Much of what we believe makes us happy does not. Happiness and contentment seem to be a lot less about having what you want, than actually wanting what you have. If I stand at the middle of the social ladder and look up at my boss' house and the car she drives, or at the mansion Scarlett O'Hara got to live in or the Ferrari a television star drives – I am never going to be happy with my house and Taurus station wagon.

However, if I can learn to adjust my vision and look back down the ladder, my home looks like a safe haven and a place of true rest next to the government sponsored low income housing across the way, or the one bedroom flats with postage stamp size yards a few streets down. And in comparison to the refugee camps of Darfur or squalor of the slums of Calcutta – those flats look like heaven.

Billions of people live down the ladder. Up the ladder sit a handful of millions. The sad reality according to David Myers, Professor of Psychology at Hope College, is this: Those of us coming from upper middle class backgrounds are LESS likely to report that we are happy than those living at lower socio-economic levels. It is part of what he terms the American paradox. Individuals who strive for wealth, tend to live with a lower sense of wellbeing.[2]

What a coincidence. The Teacher who wrote the book of the Bible called Ecclesiastes said something like that too. *If you love money and wealth, you will never be satisfied with what you have. This does not make sense either. The more you have, the more everyone expects from you. Your money will not do you any good – others will just spend it for you* (Ecclesiastes 5:10-11 CEV). It is a paradox. The more we have, the more we want. And the more we get, the less happy we are with what we have.

Myers goes on to tell of a research study done by the University of Chicago's National Opinion Research Center in which those that said they were "very happy" dropped from 35% to 30% between 1957 and 1998. The number of folks claiming they were "pretty well satisfied" with their financial situation slipped from 42% to 30%. "We excel at making a living, but fail at making a life,"[3] says Myers.

How do we compare to the rest of the world, in terms of happiness and contentment? Once you go beyond a basic threshold level—enough food to eat, decent home to live in, adequate resources for caring for one's family—more money and resources seem to add little to how happy you identify yourself to be. Once the wolf is no longer at the door—money does little to improve one's sense of contentment and sense that all is well with the world. Despite simpler lifestyles, folks living on less appear just as happy as those living with more.

What would happen if we chose to restructure our priorities? What if instead of choosing a 2000 square foot home with the RV parking along the side, we chose a 1500 square foot house with room for a tent in the loft above the garage? The results might surprise all of us. For one, it requires less hours of work to meet the mortgage and RV payments. So much less in fact, one parent could conceivably choose to stop working, or both parents could reasonably cut back. With fewer hours to work, there might be time to actually use that tent, and go away with the family for a few weeks. Not only is money saved by camping, but there might even be time to connect with the kids as you watch the sun set over the lake or burn hot dogs over the campfire.

Not a camping fan? Fear not! Stash that extra $475 a month you are saving on your home mortgage in a vacation savings account, and you can afford a week in a motel! The truth is, you just exchanged money—in terms of how much less you are paying for your mortgage—for time. You now have to work fewer hours to make that payment, so you get to spend those hours doing something you like.

As it turns out, happiness is not particularly elusive after all. It just requires discovering our priorities and then taking the necessary steps to place them in their proper order within our lives.

When asked to think of something that makes us happy, some type of image usually comes to mind. Whether it is watching a new puppy bounce around the back yard tripping over its ears; sitting squished around the Thanksgiving table with all our siblings and their kids; or huddling up on the rock hard bleachers on a crisp fall afternoon watching the local high school football game, we all know what makes us happy. Most of them involve people and family. Most of them require us to invest time in other people. In fact, most of them involve living life God's way.

The question comes down to this – how do we get there from here? The answer is simple. We need to learn to swim upstream. That is what this book is about – thinking about the value of being different. This book is about suggesting a new direction. It is about living as transformed individuals, not because we have to but because we see it as the way that brings us the greatest happiness and contentment. This book is about being people of Romans 12⁴, and about making the choice to swim upstream.

Each chapter ends with questions for further reflection, and an action step to consider. Each chapter also has an example of how a person or group chose to live differently and swim upstream. Some examples are dramatic. Most are simple. All can have a significant effect on our world if God's people choose to make them together.

Questions for further reflection:
1. Deep down, when all else is pared away, what makes you truly happy?
2. What keeps you from doing the things that make you happy?
3. Can you envision a way to change your priorities so you are able to do those things you care about more often?
4. Why do you think so many of us let the standards of others become our priorities?
5. Why is it so hard to look down the ladder at those who have less than we do, instead of up toward those who have more?

Action Plan:
- Make it a habit to spend a quiet moment each day thanking God for the gifts you have in your life, and praying for the 3 billion people across the globe that live in poverty.5
- Begin counting the hours required to work for each new purchase before you buy it, and then weigh the cost in time that will not be spent on doing the things that matter to you.

If you want to know more:
- David Myers, *The American Paradox.*
- Go to msn.com, and click on "money." There is a wealth (forgive the pun) of information here on everything from mortgage and debt calculators to stories that will help get a handle on where your money is going and how to scale back on expenses.

A Glimpse of Swimming Upstream

I consider myself a rich and happy person. If you look at my bank account *rich* would probably not be an adjective you would use to describe my financial situation. For me, being rich means that I work thirty-two hours in a week at a job I love. It allows me to enjoy the other things that are important to me—my family for instance.

Working part-time at a non-profit does not buy me a fancy car or house, but I have so many more important things in return. I am at a job that I love and I have time to be with my family. My happiness is not reflected by the job or the toys I have. For me, happiness is a way of being and by appreciating the small wonders. Abundance is all around us if we take the moment to see it. I have discovered that I do not find happiness in stuff. For me, happiness comes from spending my time the way I want and with people I love.

Tumbling Fish
Just like every other fish going with the flow.

Just who is swimming upstream these days? Christians are not looking or acting differently than the rest of the world. Like all the other fish, Christians languish in the flow of the river. This does not warm the heart of God no matter how much time we spend in worship. Christians look so much like everybody else researcher George Barna titled one of his reports *Faith Has Limited Effect on Most People's Behavior.*[6]

Think about these questions for a moment or two:

Are the people you know to be Christian any different than non-Christians in:
- The way they dress, cars they drive or houses they live in?
- The entertainment they choose?
- Their divorce rate?
- Their savings rate?
- Their indebtedness and credit card use?
- Their concern for the environment and care for all God's creation?
- The beliefs and practices they pass on to their children regarding what God says about how they live their lives?
- The amount of time and resource they invest in helping others?

With these questions I pass no judgment on divorce, Visa cards or SUV's. Personally, I am a great believer in *the one who has not sinned cast the first stone* way of living. However, the chances are that your answers to these questions indicate folks in the church look a great deal like folks not in the church. Regular church-goers seem just as likely to be over their head in credit card debt, have no savings, have just as limited time for friends, family and church, and experience just as many periods of depression, illness and unhappiness as their un-churched counterparts.

Stress, worry, and lack of contentment are as common inside the walls of our church homes as they are outside. Why is this? If we believe in the Gospel message, why does it have so little impact on how we live life?

Romans 12:1-2 says:
Dear friends, God is good. So I beg you to offer your bodies to him as a living sacrifice, pure and pleasing. That's the most sensible way to serve God. Don't be like the people of this world, but let God change the way you think. Then you will know how to do everything that is good and pleasing to him. (CEV)

Let me repeat the heart of the matter: *Do not be like the people of this world, but let God change the way you think.* Today's Christ followers are finding it harder to look like Christ's followers in a world bombarding them with 3500 marketing messages a day. They struggle to carve out an identity different from their not yet Christian friends and neighbors.

As Christians, God wants us to look like Christ – the Christ who centered his life on God, always had time for children, was there for his friends when they needed him, and challenged his followers to give freely and generously to those who did not have enough.

I will never forget running around town with a two and three year old in tow, searching for the perfect Happy Meal. I was tired of Happy Meals, but McDonalds was riding the Beanie Baby fad. Like many other unsuspecting parents, I was hauled in to the fray. Before I knew it I was driving 15 minutes out of the way to the McDonalds at the far side of town, all because they had the white seal and the restaurant closest to me only had yellow ducks. We already had yellow ducks.

I never asked myself *why it is I care if my daughters have a white seal.* The truth was they already had 25 big Beanie Babies that their grandmother gave them. They were stored in a little Plexiglas cabinet attached to their wall. My daughters did not seem to care about them all that much. Apparently, God and God's plans for me going against the flow of culture were not having much effect on my household or me.

Like me, Christians in the United States began to live in much the same way. Here is a glimpse of what those lives look like:

- Half of all new marriages in America today dissolve within the first five years. Over 85% of those divorcing say their number one problem was money.[7]
- Kids 8-17 average slightly more than a dozen trips to the mall a month, and spend an estimated $3600 a year while there.[8] At the same time, three billion people on earth live on less than two dollars a day.[9]
- Home sizes rose from an average of 750 square feet in 1950 to 2000 square feet in 1989.[10]
- Americans spent $90.93 billion on legalized gambling in 2006.[11]
- One third of all adults say financial worries prevent them from sleeping or relaxing.[12]
- Seven out of ten couples admit that financial issues are their most common conflicts.[13]
- While personal bankruptcy rates reached all time highs during the last decade, personal savings rates reached their lowest point since the Great Depression.
- The annual savings rate for 2004 was 1.8%. The last time this was lower was 1934.[14]
- While the United States makes up 5% of the world's population, it consumes between 25% and 40% of the worlds natural resources.

Are we satisfied with this picture? Is this how we want to live our lives? Are these the values we believe in and want to pass to our children?

When I asked myself these questions I found I was not happy. I was not happy that my husband and I worried about money. I was not happy I did not have much savings and I am not happy with my retirement plan. I am not happy when my daughter wandering through a mall picking up five things she just has to have, when I know they will become lost in the jungle that is her room—never to be missed nor heard from again. I was not happy that I gave no second thought to how my lifestyle affects the earth. [15]

No. . . I was not happy.

As I dug a little deeper, I discovered the road to hell was not paved with good intentions as my mother told me, but my lack of patience and need for instant gratification. So much for swimming upstream!

As any good counselor will say, the first step to solving a problem is to admit there is a problem. America has become a consumer culture. If you keep reading, we will explore the ways in which consumerism impacts each of us and our families. We will be encouraged to explore what our belief system has to say about all this, and be challenged to consider our priorities. We will be invited to swim upstream.

Questions for further reflection

1. Are you happy with your life? Are you happy with the hours you work, the sleep you get, the time you have to spend with family and friends, and the financial security you feel?
2. Read Luke 12:13-23 and 18:18-25. What do these Scriptures say to you about how God wants us to live?
3. Think of three to five Christian families you admire. In what ways do they differ from the culture around them? What Romans 12:3 differences do you note in them?
4. What do you think some of the traits of a person would be if God "changed the way they think" like Romans suggests?

Action Plan
- Imagine yourself under examination. Someone is looking for ways Christians are different from the rest of the culture. Think of one action you can faithfully implement that sets you apart from every other fish going with the flow. Write it down and tape it on your bathroom mirror. Follow through.
- Choose one of the Apostle Paul's letters in the New Testament. Read it over the next week. Make a list of the things the author talks about that would seem countercultural in our world today.

If you want to know more:
- Read Wendell Berry, *Jayber Crow.* Wendell Berry's books are famous for his discussions on living a simpler lifestyle.
- Read Wendell Berry, *That Distant Land: The Collected Stories.*
- www.Barna.org – The Barna Group does excellent, if dismaying research on the U.S. Christian church. For a glimpse of who we are, this website will provide a great perspective.

Swimming Upstream

"Credit cards were never part of my family," John says. "If Mom and Dad did not have the money, they did not buy the thing – whatever it was. When they saved enough cash for it, they would go get it. Sometimes they did not need it any longer.

"That is what made it so hard when Cindy, my fiancée, would go shopping with friends and drag out a credit card. I was appalled when I saw her credit card statements at the end of each month. Most of the items were things she did not care about once she got them home."

John sat down and talked with Cindy about her impulse spending and use of credit cards. "She did not realize how much being in debt bothered me. I never understood how my fiscal restraint seemed to her like I was a tightwad. We worked out a plan where I loosened up my standards on some consumer spending, and she uses only money we set aside for those purchases. We also decided to use credit cards only for travel and emergencies."

"I am glad we talked about this before we married," John says. "I think it would have been a tougher conversation after our wedding. Talking about money early in our relationship helped us to set priorities that make us both feel good."

Going with the flow
The rise of marketing and its impact

A thousand times a day, in a million forms, calling to us from billboards, magazines, television, radio, newspapers, movies, Websites, and telemarketers, every single message without exception is this: You are not enough. You do not have enough. You are not happy. You have not achieved the American Dream.

Wayne Muller

The lie is this: While they are promising happiness, they really are selling dissatisfaction. Our entire economy is predicated on dissatisfaction.

Wayne Muller

You don't quite know what it is you do want, but it just fairly makes your heart ache you want it so.

Mark Twain

1.3 billion people live on less than a dollar a day. 3 billion people live on less than two dollars a day.

Ron Sider

I was surprised to learn there is a science to selling. A literal science. Scientific methods and research tools are in play. Marketers study where to place an item in a store, on what shelf, and nearest to what other products.

One phenomena identified by sellers is called butt brushing.[16] It happens when the aisle is too tight and I am brushed in the butt by someone trying to pass. They have determined I am far less likely to buy their jeans because my personal space has been violated. I did not want to know that. I wanted to think I just did not like those jeans all that much.

Other tools for the seller include end caps and checkout stands, filled with impulse stuff—last minute purchases I did not know I needed until I saw it. I am kept in line long enough to get a good look at it all too, so it should not be all that surprising to see a few of those things going down the belt with the items I meant to get. I cannot call it unfair. I know the checkout counter is awash in a sea of impulse products. If I succumb, break my rules, or let my daughters add to my cart while negotiating the checkout line, it serves me right. I deserve what I get. I knew the game. I played and today I lost out to the marketers. I will try harder next time.

But a science of selling to shoppers just seems wrong somehow. That a maker of brand name jeans can hire a scientist to videotape and analyze me and the stores I shop in, and out of all that, decide exactly which spot and what shelf I am most likely to buy their jeans from—makes me feel violated and manipulated.

There is a science to selling, and retailers pay millions every year to become experts at it. That cannot possibly be good news for me. In fact, it is probably not good news for any of us. The reality is we have become a nation of consumers. We buy what we do not need with money we do not have; and then we buy bigger houses or rent storage units because we do not have enough room for it once we get it home.

A few years ago, our family moved from New York to Oregon. The housing market had tanked when we bought our home in upstate New York so we had been able to get a mortgage for a nice home. It was 2500 square feet with a full basement and the coolest octagon living room and fireplace. My girls rode their tricycles around in the basement. I loved it.

Then we moved to Oregon where all of California is also migrating. We discovered we were going to need to pay a lot more money for a lot less house. I told my realtor what I wanted to pay and he started showing me old singlewide trailers! I did what every other self respecting buyer does and began hunting ways to borrow more money so I could buy a better house. Ultimately, I pulled money from my retirement plan to get the mortgage. I do not recommend this course of action!

We purchased a simple but nice three-bedroom 1100 square foot home. I had not realized it was possible to downsize that much! We got rid of everything but the kids and the dog and moved in. Yet, within a year I was convinced we needed to add a room. There just was not enough space. I needed a place to work, the kids each needed a bedroom – there were just not enough rooms to go around. We found a contractor and went to work. A 300 square feet family room and a covered deck the size of Dodgers' stadium later—I had my addition. One year after that, I was convincing my husband we needed more room…

We built a new house. It is 1700 square feet, has three bedrooms, a family room, and is located on a great spot in a new development. That was four years ago, and last year I started talking to my husband about needing to add a sunroom…

How did we get into this mess anyway? Whatever happened to being content with what we have? I consider myself an intelligent person. I understand the rudiments of marketing, I have a basic enough grasp of finance and understand that if you keep spending more than you earn it cannot be good. I even believe there is more to life than acquiring stuff.

Furthermore, I am a committed Christian. My belief system tells me I should be okay with looking different from everyone else and that I should be willing to go against cultural patterns including keeping up with the proverbial Jones family. In fact, my beliefs tell me it is not just okay to go against the flow. It is actually expected. So why do I find myself looking so much like everyone else? Why am I buying brand name clothes and adding a sunroom? Why do I feel like I need a new cell phone the second my plan allows me to upgrade and a flat screen TV that gets a High Definition picture? I remember the days when we got one channel and it was a snowy picture, yet we parked in front of it all Saturday morning anyway. But now I refuse to watch football unless it is in HD? What happened to me?

I decided to explore that question a little. Everything was going good until we left the farm. Literally. From the time this country was founded right up until the Industrial Revolution, life was simpler. Most folks lived on small farms, and produced the majority of what they needed all by themselves. For the occasional extra—medicine, a storage barrel, candy or a book or two—excess goods produced at home could be sold, bartered or swapped. That did not leave a lot of room for surplus, and most people got by with just a few possessions. Most owned a change of clothes, a few items for their home, and grew enough food to eat. That was about it. No one thought that particularly strange as that was pretty much the standard everyone lived by.

Along came technology. Technology meant twice as many crops could be cultivated, and things that once took weeks to make by hand were quickly mass-produced at factories. Earning money in a factory meant you could buy a few things you wanted, and mass production meant there were more things to want. As early as 1901 the Thompson Redbook on Advertising was teaching would be marketers *"Advertising aims to teach people they have wants, which they did not recognize before, and where such wants can best be supplied."*[17] Crowell of Quarter Oats elaborated, *"my aim in advertising was to do educational and constructive work so as to awaken an interest and create a demand for cereal where none existed."*[18] All that advertising seems to have paid off. Tools and clothes, coffee and stoves. Eventually those evolved into cars and boats, second homes and vacations in Hawaii.

By 1950, B. Earl Puckett of Allied Stores was insisting *"It is our job to make women unhappy with what they have."*[19] Soon TV had entered the market. Now, not only could you see what the Jones family down the street was buying, you could also see what new product Joan Cleaver was using in her kitchen during the weekly *Leave it to Beaver* episode. Where magazines tapped only the niche audience that bought them, TV reached everybody. Consumerism was off and running.

Each of us wants to believe we are above all this. We think it is other people who are sucked in by glitzy advertising and smiling sales staff. Though we are exposed to an estimated 3500 ads per day-we think we avoid the trap. But more honestly, we are caught in the trap of work and spend, work and spend—and all too quickly it becomes spend and work, spend and work.

Sadly, our kids are also caught in the mess. Marketers are teaching retailers how to place products and produce TV commercials designed to catch the attention of two year olds. Any adult whose grocery cart has ever followed a toddler down the cereal aisle knows kids catch on fast. And give the advertisers credit for learning how to hook children to a brand for life. Their products are in the school soda machines, candy dispensers, or on that magical captive audience gem shown in school districts across America five days a week—Channel One News. Sponsored by beverage companies, fast food restaurants and tennis shoe makers who pay a small fortune for a thirty-second ad, the news is secondary. And why not pay a lot for such an ad? It is not as if the kids are going anywhere. No wonder our teens spend an average of $3,500 a year at the local mall![20]

It is estimated that $13 billion is spent each year marketing food and beverages that target children and youth.[21] Few of them were sponsored by the American Broccoli Association or the Vegetable Growers of America! Is it any wonder America is suffering from an epidemic of childhood obesity?

We attach value to price. So do our children. If a price is perceived as too low – we assume it cannot be good despite its real quality. When we are uninformed about a particular brand or product, often we tend to choose the mid-priced item, assuming that price signals better quality and value.

In this discussion of attaching value to price, Torstein Veblen argued in 1899 in his book *Theory of the Leisure Class*[22] that people living in wealthy societies distinguish themselves through their spending. Ironically, in *The Millionaire Next Door,*[23] Thomas Stanley and William Danko discovered that the vast majority of millionaires choose not to show off their wealth with conspicuous consumption, rather it is often the ones who do not have the big bucks who sport all the flashy stuff and get snobby about labels.

*****

Perhaps the two most significant vehicles on our road to becoming a consumer nation were the invention of the credit card, and the decision to make products that become obsolete over time.

Each speaks for itself. If I can buy it on credit, I can pay for it over time. Whether it is a house, a set of new speakers for my home sound system, or my new car – I can buy more and I make larger purchases if I can pay later. Americans took advantage of the new system in record numbers. Where in 1929 only 2% of homes had mortgages, by 1962 only 2% of the homes did not;[24] and by 2006, *Newsweek* reported Americans owed more money than they make.[25]

Planned obsolescence was the final straw. If the quality of a product was too good people held on to it too long. Bigger bucks could be made from frequent purchases by repeat customers. It did not take manufacturers long to figure out it was in their best interests to do two things—make the quality poorer so products did not last as long, and keep badgering customers with advertisements showing off the slick new and improved options now available for purchase.

And that is how I came to be drooling over a 300 square foot sunroom for my brand new 1700 square foot home.

So here is my point. As a Christian, I rightly wrestle with my values. My head tells me I care about people and critters, beautiful sunsets and standing on the dock casting a hook and worm into a placid lake. My heart tells me the AIDS epidemic in Africa and the poverty of Central America are wrong, and that God calls me to do what I can to make a difference. Knowing how I got here helps—

but the question remains, what am I going to do differently now that I know? Reality is not matching either my head or my heart. The wave of housing foreclosures, bank failures and credit crisis of 2008 all indicate our culture continues the mad dash for more possessions.

> This is what God says:
> "Simon, son of John, do you love me more than these?" Simon Peter answered, "Yes Lord, you know I do." Then feed my sheep," Jesus said. (John 21:15)

> "What will you gain if you own the whole world, but destroy yourself?" (Mark 8:36)

> "These people think religion is supposed to make you rich. And religion does make your life rich, by making you content with what you have. We did not bring anything in to this world, and we will not take anything with us when we leave. So we should be satisfied just to have food and clothes. People who want to be rich fall into all sorts of temptations and traps. They are caught in foolish and harmful desires that drag them down and destroy them. The love of money causes all kinds of trouble. Some people want money so much that they have given up their faith and caused themselves a lot of pain." (1 Timothy 6:5b-10)

"Warn the rich people of the world not to be proud or to trust in wealth that is easily lost. Tell them to have faith in God who is rich and blesses us with everything we need to enjoy life. Instruct them to do as many good deeds as they can and to help everyone. Remind the rich to be generous and share what they have. (1 Timothy 6:17-18)

And this is what culture says:

"Buy that new car; you deserve to ride in luxury."

"Take that trip to the exclusive beach getaway for adults only. You work hard, so enjoy some pampering."

"Look after yourself first, it's a dog eat dog world. No one else is going to worry about you if you don't."

"Live for today. You never know what might happen tomorrow."

The difference is stark. Where do my values fit, and in which belief system will I trust—God's or the world's?

Questions for further reflection

1. Describe a time you felt reeled in by a salesperson or marketing campaign. Why do you think you let them convince you to make the purchase?
2. Do you think consumerism is a cultural problem? Whom does consumerism affect, and how does it affect them?
3. Do you have any favorite brands? How and why did they become your favorite brands?
4. In what ways do you see our culture at odds with what God has to say?
5. Think of a purchase you just had to have. How did you feel about it after you bought it? How did you feel about it a year later?

Action Plan

•   Watch five TV commercials. Write down the promises made in the ads. What messages are behind the actual ad campaign?
•   Make next month a no excess purchase month. Avoid the mall and shopping centers, and ignore advertisements. Invest the time you would normally spend shopping in doing something with a family member or friend. Write your reflections and share them as a family.

If you want to know more:
- Read Craig L. Blomberg, *Heart, Soul and Money*
- Read Juliet B. Schor, *The Overspent American*
- Read Paco Underhill, *Why We Buy: The Science of Shopping*

Swimming Upstream

"I remember that you refused to purchase those Air Jordans for me, Mom," Kyle said. "Although, I think it came across as a lesson in the value of money rather than a stand against big business."

In 1990, Kyle was ten years old, and one of eleven boys in his Sunday school class. That was the same year that the Air Jordan VI athletic shoe was released. As Kyle's mother, I viewed Air Jordan VI as much more than an expensive $120 sneaker marketed to the ego needs of pre-teen boys. A key issue was paying this much for sneakers when they would be outgrown in several months.

One evening at craft night, a monthly gathering of women, some of whom were also the mothers of boys in Kyle's Sunday school class; a what-if question was posed. What if we refused to buy these expensive sneakers for our boys? What if we could subvert their insistence on this purchase by agreeing among ourselves to cap our sneaker price at $60? Would this approach diffuse the peer pressure? If we named one another in the conversations with our sons, that is, "Did you know that Dwane's mom is not spending more than $60 for his sneakers? He's not getting Air Jordan's either." Would that settle the issue with our sons?

That year several mothers took a stand against buying expensive sneakers. Working together empowered us to be more matter-of-fact in our dealings with our children, and helped us eliminate social acceptance as a motivator for the kind of sneaker that would be bought.

Kyle, now age twenty-eight, says, "I eventually got my pair of Air Jordans, but I had to go through Grandma to do it. Thank goodness for birthday shopping!" Kyle adds a side note. "When they got wet they were the stinkiest shoes I have ever owned. I never bought another pair of overpriced sneakers again."

Keeping the water clean for swimming
Creation Care

We didn't create this world, but we are busy de-creating it.

Bill McKibbon[26]

The earth has enough for everyone's need, but not everyone's greed.

Mahatma Gandhi

We recently entered a new century, but we also are entering a new world, one where the collisions between our demands and the earth's capacity to satisfy them are becoming daily events. It may be another crop- withering heat wave, another village abandoned because of invading sand dunes, or another aquifer pumped dry. If we do not act quickly to reverse the trends, these seemingly isolated events will come more and more frequently, accumulating and combining to determine our future.

No economy, however technologically advanced, can survive the collapse of its environmental support system.

Lester Brown

Everybody's business (conservation) became nobody's business.

David G. Myers

Only when the last tree has died and the last river been poisoned and the last fish been caught will we realize we cannot eat money.

Cree Indian Proverb

They call it *the tragedy of the commons*. I had never heard of that before. Ecologist Garrett Hardin coined it, and what it means is if it belongs to everybody, do not expect anybody to take responsibility for it, especially in a world that honors individualism and is heavily invested in self-interest.

I ran into this in my housing development awhile back. Clauses were written right into the development's covenants that require us to maintain our properties in certain uniform ways. Having grown up in a rural environment, one where a good lawn generally just meant a lawn the cows were kept from—I found the covenants a little annoying at first. I wanted a Birch tree as my street tree. I have always loved White Birch, and since we finally built a place of our own and were starting from scratch—I wanted one on my front lawn. I am not allowed to have a White Birch as a street tree. The developer who plotted these houses and wrote the codes had either a thing for Armstrong Maple and for continuity, or a thing against White Birch. I was required to plant two Armstrong Maple trees where my property borders the street. They are beautiful trees but I wanted a White Birch.

The reasoning is that if we all abide by the rules, set certain standards and then maintain them, everyone will benefit. Common trees planted at roughly the same time reach maturity at roughly the same time. The neighborhood looks neat and orderly. It looks like we take care of our stuff—as if we are good neighbors. As the neighborhood looks improve so do the values of the neighborhood homes. There are aesthetic and financial benefits for us when we keep the neighborhood tidy.

It is in this environment that I learned about the tragedy of the commons. Our neighborhood has two common areas. One is a long stretch of property adjacent to the city bike path perfect for kids to play soccer or dogs to fetch a ball. The other borders a small pond. Toddlers in strollers and youth with fishing poles are found there, watching the ducks on the water or trying to convince a bass to run with the fishhook. Both areas are nice, and add value to our home.

Since no one actually owns them, however, no one actually wants to care for them. Water bottles, candy wrappers, Coke cans and Wal-Mart bags are left behind when the people make their way home. The long field gets the worst of it. The city owns the land and keeps the grass mowed. Thus, the field is ideal for dog walking. Many dogs and their owners make themselves quite at home. Most seem to forget those handy little bags for carrying Rover's poop to the family trash can. Consequently, dodging brown piles deters most soccer games, and few fans are willing to risk the penalty of an overly physical game of touch football. The dogs, thanks to the irresponsibility of their owners, have the field pretty much to themselves.

When a plea went out in our sporadically published development newsletter to spruce the commons up on a fall Saturday only a handful came—mostly board members. The tragedy of the commons—when an area is the responsibility of everybody, it is the responsibility of nobody. I did not make the mess. Why should I clean it up? I do not have a dog. I do not like to play soccer anyway. It is those d__ kids. Parents do not teach them to pick up after themselves anymore.

While we all can see the problem if every dog used this spot to relieve themselves, few of us can see the problem when our dog does it just this one time. Sadly, I remember rationalizing that argument in my own head on one cold, rainy walk last year.

The tragedy continues.

The world is beginning to face some hard decisions about the things we hold as common. What freely belongs to everybody has tragically been the responsibility of nobody. Potential disaster has been happening so slowly, most of us do not realize we are almost at boiling point. What did not seem to matter when just a few of us did them becomes disastrous when the whole world wants to do the same.

Water is a case in point. For many of us in North America water simply exists. When we need it, we find it. The city brings it to our door, the well driller taps into it below our feet, or the pipes bring it from a nearby reservoir. Gone are the days where we located our farms, cattle ranches and our towns around rivers and streams, lakes and ponds. Water sources used to be the determining factor on everything. Without water readily at hand, we simply moved on until we found a better place.

Life revolves around the rhythm of water. I remember my grandfather's farm well. It was 325 acres of gently rolling hills, surrounding a few large fields for crops. He ran a small dairy herd on the place owned by his family from the time when it was purchased from the Native Americans. There were three water sources on the farm. The young stock lived in the shed by the deep pond. When calves were big enough to leave the main barn, they were walked across the road and put in the pen by that pond.

The cows not producing milk were put in the pasture with the second pond. They came and went as they pleased until they were ready to give birth. As they made their way to the water several times a day, Grandpa kept track of them, watching for signs they would be dropping their calves. The main herd was housed in pasture with a big wet spot where the water level varied with the weather. They got all the water they cared about. When first purchased, all of life revolved around those ponds on the farm.

The rhythm changed with wealth and technology. Two wells were drilled—one for the barn and one for the house. Water was so abundant that my parents and my Aunt and Uncle were given a few acres. Two more houses were added to the property. When Grandpa passed away, like many a small farm in upstate New York, neither son nor son-in-law, not grandson nor daughter, wanted the eighteen-hour days that went with farm life. No one wanted to "marry those darn cows" I remember overhearing one night. The farm, despite my mother's broken heart, went to a developer. Five houses now occupy the area, with more planned.

This story frequently replicates across North America. Farmlands and deserts alike, have given way to suburbia as we chase the sun. In the process, we failed to answer some hard questions. What about the water? What about the two ponds and a wet spot? Communities sprang up where only nomads lived in the past. Millions now live on land that once supported small tribes migrating from spring to spring, following the flow of the water. Now we read stories about cities running out of water and states fighting over water rights.

Technology made it possible. Water is pumped from once mighty rivers, so lawns can be watered and golf courses built; schools established and trees planted; in an environment previously unable to sustain life.

The results are beginning to unfold—specifically an ever-increasing shortage of water. 70% of all the water drawn from these rivers and aquifers irrigates 670 million acres of farmland that grows the earth's food.[29] While the globe increasingly has been fed – it has been at the expense of its rivers.[30] The Aral Sea provides a sad example of the reality we will eventually face. It has all but disappeared.

I would like to plead ignorance. I would like to point out I never personally lived on a spot without sustainable water, and that I never personally abused the resource. I took just as many hot showers as you, watered my lawn just as long, washed my car just as many times, and flushed the toilet just as often. I did it all without ever giving it a second thought. Water sustainability never crossed my mind. It did not seem important.

It needs to. Ignorance will not be an excuse.

God tells us that I am to be a partner in caring for all that God created (Genesis 9:1-11). In doing this, what clues do we have about keeping resources sustainable? Once again, quite a lot once I started to pay attention. I am to be a partner in caring for all God has created. I am to be a manager—a steward. The culture is driving me to master all that God created, controlling it for my use, while the Lord calls me to care for it—to make room for all God's creatures to flourish.

It did not matter to me before. With so many people and not so many resources, I know now I need to spend more time discerning what God expects from our partnership to manage well all that the Lord created.

Questions for further reflection:
1. What do you see as the greatest obstacle to caring for creation?
2. Can you think of a time when you have observed the "tragedy of the commons?" Were you able to make a difference?
3. Read these Scripture passages: Psalm 24:1-6; Haggai 1:5,6; Luke 19:12-27. What do you hear the Lord saying to you in these readings?

Action Plan
- Change the light bulbs in your house to Energy Star models. According to the US government website (energystar.gov) "If every American home replaced just one light bulb with an Energy Star qualified bulb, we would save enough energy to light more than three million homes for a year, more than $600 million in annual energy costs, and prevent greenhouse gases equivalent to the emissions of more than 800,000 cars." – energystar.gov (energystar.gov/index.cfm?c=cfls.pr_cfls)
- Get educated. Pick an area of the environment that is of interest to you – water resources, melting glaciers, rain forests, etc. – and learn more about it. What reasonable solutions do you see offered? In what small ways can you begin to live differently?

If you want to know more:
- Read Lester Brown's, *Plan B 2.0* (see the end notes to this chapter)
- Read anything written by Wendell Berry—any of his works or stories. Wendell reminds us of the beauty in

simplicity, and the joy that can be found in working *with* nature
* Set your browser to www.earthwatch.org or www. earth-policy.org.

Swimming upstream

"It seems like such a small thing," Martha told me. "Using cloth shopping bags does not seem like it would make much of a difference. Then I took a mission trip to Mexico, and saw all the plastic grocery bags flying around. When I commented about it to the missionary family with whom we stayed, they told me it is a huge problem. The city grew so quickly that basic services like sanitation are not available. There is simply no place to put all the trash.

"That got me to thinking about where the plastic goes in my home country. When I discovered the estimate that the United States uses one hundred billion plastic bags a year,[31] I realized the problem exists here too. We just have landfills to hide ours better!"

"The solution is simple. I purchased a dozen reusable cloth bags and I store a bunch in our vehicles. Each time I go to the store, I grab enough for what I plan to purchase. It has worked so well that I started buying them for my friends who are not using them yet. Why waste natural resources when I can buy a sturdy bag and use it for years? Each time I see a plastic bag blowing down the highway, I remember why I go to the effort of using my own cloth bags."

Sick Little Fishes
Going with the flow can be bad for your health

> Never before has one generation of American teenagers
> been less healthy, less cared for, or less prepared for life
> than their parents were at the same age.
>> National Assoc. of School Boards of Education,
>> 1990 report

> There is more to life than merely increasing its speed.
>> Mahatma Gandhi

> The greatest wealth is health.
>> Virgil

> Health is a state of complete physical, mental and social
> well-being, and not merely the absence of disease or
> infirmity.
>> World Health Organization

> Diseases of the soul are more dangerous and more
> numerous than those of the body.
>> Cicero

> My own prescription for health is less paperwork and
> more running barefoot through the grass.
>> Leslie Grimutter

Few adages seem to share more truth than the one about good health—we do not really notice what we have until we lose it. For instance, my church is in the midst of a devastating time. Four of our church members who routinely fill core leadership roles are experiencing devastating illnesses within their families. Several more families are fighting debilitating disease. As a congregation, we have been forced to give health and wellbeing a far more intimate look than ever before. It is painful—no pun intended.

Good health. Anything seems possible with it and everything seems like a mountain to climb without it. Living is easier when good health greets us every morning. Few couples go through pregnancy without saying at least a half dozen times "I don't care if it is a boy or a girl, just as long as the baby is healthy."

Good health has come to mean more to my family too. My husband was diagnosed with Rheumatoid Arthritis in 2007. It did not take us long to discover why so many in the medical community are beginning to call it rheumatoid disease instead of arthritis as its impact can be dramatic. The visual picture of arthritis—suffering from aches and pains—bears little resemblance to what my husband experiences: no energy and many headaches, flu like symptoms and side effects from a never-ending series of nasty drugs. Each morning is an adventure. It is a bit like *Where's Waldo?* We never know which joint will hurt when my husband first opens his eyes to greet a new day.

When we first heard the word arthritis we were relieved. A number of other scary options were on the table. Arthritis sounded so benign next to the other possibilities. Sometimes ignorance really is bliss! Well into it now, we are beginning to get the hang of the disease. It has not been easy. We did not expect to be giving health a second thought in our early forties, especially when we work out daily and eat all the right foods. Silly us.

As a nation, more of us are beginning to give our health more than a passing glance. Ironically, if we all know health is such a critical ingredient to live the kind of life we want, why do we do so many things to put health at risk? Our diet provides a great case in point.

When I was growing up, dining out created memories because they were such a novelty. There were several reasons for eating out so infrequently. First, there was not a lot of extra money. Even with cheap kids meals many families still considered restaurants a luxury. Second, even if we could afford it, why bother? Mom's food tasted just as good and it would be ready when Dad walked in the door from work anyway. With all the free child labor weeding the garden all summer long, why not stay home and eat our own food?

The fast food industry was born during my lifetime, and I witnessed all the changes it brought. More moms entered the work force, and lifestyles got busier for even the youngest members of the family. It became normal to swing through the drive-up and grab a bucket of chicken on the way home, or a few happy meals and some burgers on the way to the ballgame. Where Americans once ate out every one in ten meals, we now do so closer to one in three.[32] Along the way, we failed to ask, "Is this food actually good for me?" Fast lives required fast food, and that was that. The age of societal obesity and heart disease was ushered in. Stadium seats and the average blue jean waist size got larger as the American derrière grew in size. Clothing manufacturers adjusted their sizes to make us feel OK about the changes, and the old size 10 became the new size 8. The fact remains however, Americans got bigger and our health became worse.

Added to the problems caused by an overabundance of processed foods, and too few fruits and vegetables, are issues of increased stress and less sleep. As both parents worked more hours outside the home, household chores became harder to fit into overwhelming schedules. Sleep became the first casualty, as evenings got filled up with loads of laundry, house cleaning and bill paying – chores formerly covered during the day or on weekends.[33] By the time a parent could relax, they were too wide-awake to sleep.

Throw into this mix the stress that accompanies running from one activity to the next. Thirty percent of adults say they experience high stress every day, and one third of the population admits they are rushed to do the things they have to do.[34] Do we need to wonder why increased rates of blood pressure and stomach ailments have given birth to completely new profit centers for pharmaceutical companies?

As the speed of American life increased, so did rates of depression. Among Americans born since WWII, depression has increased tenfold. Though individualistic countries have higher numbers of people whom claim they are "very happy," higher suicide and homicide rates also seem to come with the territory.[35] Preoccupied with our own lives, we lost our concern for community and the sense of belonging it gave us. Teens feel the pinch as jobs, school, interests and friends compete for their time. All this tension and depression add to the health issues—bringing the cycle full circle. No matter how we define depression, young people in the United States have grown up with more affluence but are less happy. They experience significantly greater risks of depression and higher rates of suicide. "Never has a culture experienced such physical comfort combined with such psychological misery."[36] So much for Proverbs and "Train a child in the way they should go."[37]

So why do we remain on the treadmill? If fast lives and fast food lead to cancer and heart disease, obesity, depression and incredibly unhappy children, why are we so slow to change our patterns? God had a different blueprint in mind for our lives, and it may be time for us to look more closely at what that kind of life might be like. It might be time for some Romans 12 thinking— time for some swimming upstream.

Consider these words from Scripture:

"Come to me, all you who are weary and burdened, and I will give you rest. Take my yoke upon you and learn from me, for I am gentle and humble in heart, and you will find rest for your souls. For my yoke is easy and my burden is light."

Matthew 11:28-30 (NIV)

An expert in the Law of Moses stood up and asked Jesus a question to see what he would say. "Teacher," he asked, "what must I do to have eternal life?" Jesus answered, "What is written in the Scriptures? How do you understand them?" The man replied, "The Scriptures say, 'Love the Lord your God with all your heart, soul, strength and mind.' They also say 'Love your neighbor as you love yourself.'" Jesus said, "You have given the right answer. If you do this, you will have eternal life."

Luke 10: 25-28 (CEV)

Mark Twain is reported to have said, *"It ain't those parts of the Bible that I can't understand that bother me, it is the parts that I do understand."* He put it as well as anyone. It is not hard to understand what Jesus said to the Teacher of the Law in the Luke passage above. Were Jesus to say it today it might sound a little like this: "If you are tired and the ways of the world have left you overwhelmed—come to me. My plan for you was not to spend your time looking inward and striving for personal success anyway. My plan for you was to focus on others and invest in them. The world says love yourself. I say love your neighbor."

If stress, poor physical and mental health, and lack of sleep get us down – maybe we have got our sights aimed at the wrong target. Maybe we are living by the wrong rules. Maybe life really is as simple as loving God and loving our neighbor.

> *"Since the 1960's Americans have been soaring materially, and until recently, sinking socially. We enjoy unprecedented peace and prosperity, liberty and longevity, technology and tolerance...And we have more children of children, more suicidal and violent teens, more demoralized and incarcerated adults, diminished civility and trust, and fewer and unhappier marriages."*[38]

Our physical and mental health tries to get our attention. Our souls yearn for a different way of life. Romans 12 provides the answer. Stop looking to the ways of the world if you want to find a better life. Consuming more will not make you happy. If you want to be content, move closer to God's way. It is time to act differently than the rest of the world. It is time to swim upstream.

Though the solution might seem oversimplified, beginning to worry more about someone else really does make a difference in our attitudes and outlook. Investing in other people brings happiness and wellbeing. People who can name several close friends live with greater health and happiness.[39]

My Grandmother had a great spirit of adventure. Though being married to a farmer meant she rarely left home, she would talk about her fishing trip to Alaska, and the places she had yet to see. I remember several conversations about the landmarks she hoped to visit, and the states she planned to investigate.

My Grandfather, on the other hand, was happiest at home on the dairy farm surrounded by his land and his critters. It was a family joke. Grandpa and Grandma would drive over for a Sunday afternoon visit. Cards would be shuffled and pinochle hands dealt, and the conversations would flow. We discussed the previous week and what the grandkids were doing. We talked about the involvements of aunt, uncle and cousins, who died, and who had a new girlfriend, car or job. Then, like a lightning bolt out of the blue, Grandpa would stand up, grab his coat and head for the door. He had stayed long enough and was ready for home. There was no winding down of conversation, no jingling car keys and no warning. He just searched for his hat and started walking. Grandma was left with little to do other than say goodbye and follow his retreating back.

As Grandpa got older his habits became more set. While Grandma would talk of retirement as a time to see the places on her list, Grandpa seldom expressed interest. Though Grandma convinced him to fly to Florida once, the handwriting seemed to be on the wall when he chose to buy a car and drive home rather than use their return ticket. And that was that. It was the only trip I remember them taking outside New York State.

As Grandpa's health declined, Grandma would sometimes talk of the places she would visit someday. His illness left little doubt there would be years spent alone so she kept her dreams alive. Fishing trips and friends far away still held appeal for her. Senior bus tours sounded like a hoot. She was going to explore the world.

Why she never did remains a mystery to me. She lived another 6 years after my Grandfather passed away and saw both my children born, her seventh and eighth great-grandchildren. She remained in good health and could quite easily have taken any of those trips. Instead, we watched her increasingly draw into herself. Without my Grandfather to share life, her dreams held less appeal. Despite their differences she was lost without him. Without the need to fix him breakfast, she found little reason to get out of bed herself. I remain sad that she did not have a close friend in addition to Grandpa or did not become involved in the community. Instead, her life revolved around Grandpa, the farm and her family. The farm was sold in their retirement because their children had lives of their own. She had little to hang on to when my Grandfather passed away.

Each of us needs other people to make our lives whole. Good friends and taking part in a community and a family gives us purpose outside ourselves. Christ makes it clear, a willingness to be humble and a heart for our neighbors will serve us well.[40]

Good health means letting people in. It means caring as much about others as ourselves, and investing time in our relationships. It also means evaluating how we spend our time, and what we eat and drink.

When my kids look back, what will they remember? Will another trip through the drive-up window on the way to the soccer field seem a fair exchange for making dinner together, and sitting around the table chattering as a family? Will they notice I was not there as much as they wanted, or give me a pass because I was busy building their college fund? Will they wish I had stopped working when I walked in the door at night, and invested a little more time in asking about their day?

Good health includes good relationships. God knows this and tells us to love our neighbors as ourselves.

Questions for further reflection:
1. Who was your best friend as a child? What are the things you shared between you?
2. Can you think of a person who lives this principle of loving and investing in others? Can you remember a scenario where selfishness did not result in happiness? What happened?
3. Gandhi said, "There is more to life than increasing its speed." Does the speed of life affect you, and your sense of happiness and wellbeing?
4. What have you learned about Jesus calling us to love our neighbors as we love ourselves?

Action Plan
- Turn a family meal or friends get together into an event. Involve everybody. Pick a fun dish with something for everyone to do, decorate the table, and use the preparation time enjoying each other. 'If I was stuck on a desert isle, I'd take three things . . ."
- Pick two nights a week and declare them work free zones. Commit to leaving work at the doorstep when you arrive home, and leave the computer off. Let the cell phone go to voicemail. Focus the evening on strengthened relationships with family and friends.
- Instead of focusing on yourself or your stuff, consider volunteering in a food program, giving a caregiver a needed afternoon off, visiting a lonely neighbor or volunteering time in a children or youth program. If you keep a journal, record your insights.

If you want to know more:
- David Myers, *The American Paradox*
- Craig Blomberg, *Neither Poverty Nor Riches*
- Wayne Muller, *Sabbath: Finding Rest, Renewal and Delight in Our Busy Lives.*
- The Stewardship Series of books available from Mennonite Mutual Aid, especially *Time Warped* by Steve Ganger.

Swimming Upstream
Dean says, "My schedule was so far out of hand I was anxious every time I looked at my calendar. It was filled to the brim. I felt so guilty because there were so many things I wanted to spend time on but could not see where to fit it all. When events like a ball game or band concert came up for my kids, I would try to get there for part of it. There was never any time to take them to a movie or go out to dinner with my wife. It really started to affect my mental health. I felt down all the time because I thought my priorities were all messed up. I could not see any way to change it for the better.

"That was when my friend shared an idea that worked for him. Starting with a day or two each month, he slowly began to block out time for his family. He would write 'meeting with JRC' on a weeknight—the initials of his son. Then in the next week, his wife's initials were added to a block of time around breakfast. He went into the office late, and spent a little extra time at home with his spouse. Over time, he began to spend intentional time with the people who mattered most to him.

"Now I do the same thing. It took me awhile to get intentional time carved out of each week, but I am finally there. The thing I found most amazing is that my calendar is still just as full but I am not anxious about it anymore. Now I know it includes my priorities. I get just as much done but I found time to include the people I care about every week too. I feel a lot better about my life!"

The Richest Fish in the Sea
Money, money, money. America's new God.

We can tell our values by looking at our checkbook stubs.

Gloria Steinem

The real measure of your wealth is how much you'd be worth if you lost all your money.

Author Unknown

When I have money, I get rid of it quickly, lest it find a way into my heart.

John Wesley

Money is like manure. You have to spread it around or it smells.

J. Paul Getty

When you let money speak for you, it drowns out anything else you meant to say.

Mignon McLaughlin

A man is usually more careful of his money than of his principles.

Oliver Wendell Holmes, Jr.

By all accounts, Americans are among the richest fish in the sea. Though not all of us are wealthy, few ever face real concerns about starvation. A myriad of social programs and safety nets exist to help our poor find food, medical help and other services. In fact when stacked up against those living in poverty in much of the world, our poor seem quite well off.

Money. We have it. By worldly standards, we have a lot of it. Even so, many of us spend a lot of time dreaming about how to get more, and then how to spend it once we get it. We even spend it before we have it. For years, I dreamt of striking it rich and becoming a multi-millionaire. I am almost ashamed to share just how much thought I put into this because I have gone so far as to plan everything I would do with it.

First, I would set aside money for my daughters' college education. Then I would give family members $300,000 to pay off their mortgages. Then I would take one million and set it aside for my family to guarantee a comfortable lifestyle. All the rest would go to a charitable foundation. In my dream, my family and I spend the rest of our lives giving it away.

I like money. I like what it can buy for me, and the way it eases my life. I like the calm that comes when I have enough of it for the monthly bills, and conversely, and I hate the months where I worry about how to stretch it far enough. As biblical stewardship author Mark L. Vincent writes, it has a god-like quality.[41] It takes effort to keep myself from worshipping it.

In each job I have held, I was positive that if I earned just a little more my life would be so much easier. At first, I was a teacher and worked in a small school in rural New York State. By most standards, we were underpaid. My starting salary was $9000. Even in the 1980's it did not stretch very far. I have vivid memories of totaling my two monthly paychecks, then jotting down every bill I expected that month, subtracting each bill from the total. Then I would figure out what I was going to do to bring in more income for the month. The bills always outpaced the paychecks.

I started waitressing on the side. When I started earning more as a waitress on a good weekend than as a teacher with a Master's degree, I lost some enthusiasm for teaching. Ironically, my teacher's union passed a contract the same year I left teaching that would have given me a 33% raise, but by then I was feeling a call into camping ministry. I started my new job with a paycheck 60% higher than when I was teaching. The routine was the same though—add the two paychecks, subtract the monthly bills and figure out how to cover the gap. Even though I was making more money, I never had enough.

In my defense, it was not because I was a big spender. By the time the camping career began, Uncle Sam wanted my monthly payment for all the loans he had given me toward my degrees. That and my first daughter was going through disposable diapers and formula at a pace few parents ever see coming. Since my husband was a full time student, it was not an illusion. We really were broke!

Fortunately for me, the denomination I worked for was committed to its employees. Significant raises came often in those first five years. None of the raises seemed to be enough, though. Because we were so strapped for cash with our baby and one of us was a fulltime student, we started my camping career taking my retirement benefit as cash instead of putting it into my retirement account. Food on the table today seemed more important than a comfortable retirement forty years later. I cannot tell you how many times I have wished to take that decision back now that I know the glory of compound interest, the importance of investing early and am twenty years closer to retirement.

My first raises went to paying for school outright, rather than acquiring more government loans. Later we began investing the money for retirement into the retirement account as intended.

The truth is this, however. Once we arrived at break even, no new raise ever seemed to mean any left over money. There was always something new that we needed and it always seemed legitimate. First, it was a bigger car because the back seat was small when it came time to add a second car seat. Then it was a house. Although our singlewide trailer may have seemed cozy when we were childless, it was definitely feeling crowed with two little ones running around. Once we owned a house the water heater died, the furnace quit and the monster sized back deck rotted through. The cost of electricity sharply increased. The heating bill doubled.

What I now know is this: ***There will never be enough money if I cannot figure out the difference between wants and needs.***

After all this time, I know myself pretty well. I have many wants. Every Sunday paper advertizing section and every stroll through the mall is going to help me discover a dozen new wants to add to my already long list. When I am honest, though, I realize my needs are few. I need a place to live and some warmth. I need some food to eat and clean water to drink. I need clothes, my family and some good friends that care if I wake up in the morning. I need purpose in life to get me out of bed to meet each new day. While I may want a Porsche, any reliable transportation will get me where I need to go. And though the very thought of adding that sunroom to my house can help me waste an hour in daydreams, my home is beyond adequate already.

Until I get past equating money with things I want, I will never have money left over. Until I have money left over I will not have peace of mind. I will never be as generous as I think God invites me to be. I will always focus on money as if it is mine. I will always struggle with the reality that it is all Gods and God has blessed me generously.

I do not think I am alone in struggling with the god-like power of money. Money has become an idol for many of us. We chase after its golden ring. We dream of having more, and frequently spend it before we have even earned it. Money drives our thoughts, words and actions. We lie, cheat or steal to get more of it.

Going with the flow of culture was a bad idea for me. It lulled me into cranking up my lifestyle to a point where I must either work a certain number of hours or start selling some of my things. I lay awake at night feeling the stress of a trying to accomplish too much in too few hours.

As a follower of Christ, the going gets tough at this point. God's people have in their possession, all the money to fund God's *entire* ministry. According to Emptytomb.org, if Americans who identify with the church increased their giving to an average of 10% of income, there could be an additional $164 billion given to the church. If 60% of this amount were made available to expand overseas missions activity, that number would mean an additional $98 billion available for overseas missions.[42] And with that other 40% left here in the United States, folks like me trying to fund worthy ministries such as reaching our kids for Christ, might be able to sleep through a lot more nights!

It is a painful process, but I believe God asks me to enter the wrestling ring:

- Though the Bible suggests that a tithe starts at 10% and rises from there, the average Christian returns significantly less to the work of the Kingdom.[43] The line between wants and needs has all but disappeared.

- Intentionally teaching stewardship, that is, teaching people what God says about what we do with everything God gives us, is disappearing. Pastors are routinely reminded, "My money is my business—not the church's." Pastors routinely say, "I never talk about money."
- Although between 75-80% of us say this country is too materialistic,[44] *"overall half the population in the richest country in the world says they cannot afford everything they need. And it is not just the poorer half."*[45] Our belief system has very little impact on our use of money, possessions and time.[46]
- Americans spend $24.3 billion on candy, $64 billion on soft drink, $354 billion on going out to eat, $85 billion on lawn care and gardening, $38 billion on state lotteries, and $31 billion on pets each year. At the same time it is projected that $98 billion would eradicate preventable childhood deaths under five, provide access to basic health and education to the world's poor, and even leave $1 billion for global evangelism.[47]

If I want to swim upstream, I must do a better job of considering my neighbor's ability to eat, receive basic health care and education against my list of wants. If I really believe God's incredible abundance provides enough; if that is not just some line I keep repeating to myself once a year when it is time to make a financial commitment to my church, I must learn to share with my neighbor. While I am tempted to focus on all the people who are less generous than me—I hear God saying get the log out of your own eye before you try to remove the speck from anyone else's.[48]

I believe God gives us mentors who can help us wrestle with how our wants stack up against our needs. Three persons from my American Baptist tradition come to mind. Marian Boehr graduated from the top of her class at medical school and could have become wealthy practicing medicine anywhere in the United States. Instead, she spent many years serving the poor in India, often using what little salary she did receive to buy supplies for the hospital.

Edy McCarty was a teacher in her early thirties when she felt a call to the mission field. She spent her missions career serving in Thailand.

Maurice Miller worked as a pastor all his life, mostly at the local church level, including more than a decade at our camp here in Oregon. Serving mostly small congregations, he did not accumulate great wealth. Even so, I have rarely seen a person so quick to give generously to a ministry where he was passionate—camping in this case. He and his wife not only gave significant amounts of their time through the years, they also gave lavishly from their checkbook in a way few others equal.

Each person turned their back on many things most of us would see as necessities. Edy and Marian battled heat, poverty and social injustices in another culture. Maurice rarely took his eyes off reaching children for Christ. While they accumulated little in terms of the material world, all three taught me much about treasure storing in the kingdom of heaven. They are my heroes. They offer me examples of how to swim upstream.

If we have so much when compared to the rest of the cultures existing on earth today, why do we always feel like it is not enough? Is having more worth all the effort of more hours worked, fewer hours spent with family and friends, and more hungry people across the globe as I accumulate more stuff for myself? At best, I am treading water in a culture we created. God is challenging me to work a lot harder to swim against the current, and my global neighbors hope I learn to do it soon.

Questions for further reflection:
1. What are the most important things in life for you? Make a list. In what ways does money affect each of these positively or negatively?
2. Read Luke 14: 12-14. What do you hear God saying to you? Can you think of a time you have seen someone living out this Scripture?
3. Matthew 19:29 says, "All who have given up home or brothers and sisters or father and mother or children or land for me will be given a hundred times as much. They will also have eternal life." Discuss this Scripture in light of Matthew 19:24 "In fact, it's easier for a camel to go through the eye of a needle than for a rich person to get into God's kingdom."

4. Why do you believe Christians have such a hard time with the concept of a tithe, and giving generously from their finances?

Action Plan

- Put God to the test. For a two-month period, give the first 10% of your income to God for God's work. Keep a journal through the two months noting the ways in which God took care of your needs. Were you able to pay all your bills and meet all your financial obligations? What did you give up in order to give generously to God? Did you receive anything in return during these two months?
- Read Malachi 3 each day for one week. After the reading, sit in silent meditation for ten minutes and listen for what God is saying to you. Keep a journal, noting what you hear, and what you feel in the encounter with this Scripture passage.

If you want to know more:

- www.emptytomb.org
- ww.financialseminary.org (or anything by Christian financial ethicist Gary Moore).
- Marian Boehr, *Medicine and Miracles amid the Multitudes,* International Ministries American Baptist Foreign Missions Society, 2002.
- Ronald J. Sider, *Rich Christians in the Age of Hunger*
- Read a biography of Mother Theresa or any other person who focused their life on living out Micah 6:8.

Swimming Upstream

"I hate to admit it, but I started tithing because of guilt," Susan shared. "I was sitting with a group of fellow clergy. All of them were middle aged or older, and all of them were sharing stories about tithing. Some were talking about how they felt it was important to lead by example, so they routinely shared with their congregation their own beliefs about giving. Others told stories of how God blessed their efforts to give away ten percent of all they received. One even told the story of how God had blessed him so well in retirement that he was giving away far more than 10%.

"Each of these stories made me painfully aware of my own lack of tithing. With a massive seminary loan and a small child at home, I just could not fathom how I could stretch the salary from my small church any further. While I gave to the church weekly, I did not see a way to give 10%. Listening to all my colleagues, I felt called to follow the preaching of Malachi 3, and put God to the test.

"That was a long time ago, but I can honestly say this it was the greatest leap of faith I ever took. I never missed the additional money, but the real blessing was one in my heart. God changed my heart through the process. What I could do for God and God's kingdom became far more important to me than money. It just feels good to be generous! God has given me so much—my family, my home, my health.

"That colleague group changed my life. It helped me take my focus off money, and center it on the Lord."

Swim, swim, swim
What if I just want time to float?

Millions long for immortality who do not know what to do with themselves on a rainy Sunday afternoon.

Susan Ertz

We always have enough time if we but use it right.

Johann Wolfgang von Gothe

Everything on earth has its own time and its own season. There is a time for birth and death, planting and reaping, for killing and healing, destroying and building, for crying and laughing, weeping and dancing, for throwing stones and gathering stones, embracing and parting. There is a time for finding and losing, keeping and grieving, for tearing and sewing, listening and speaking. There is also time for love and hate, for war and peace.

Ecclesiastes 3:1-8

The problem is not simply that we work too much, So, when we are moving faster and faster, the problem is that we are working for the wrong reward.

Walter Muller

Christmas is one of my favorite times of year. For me, it is not about the stuff—honest. I am not that big on getting gifts. I do not like being the center of attention, and I never feel like I say the right things in response to the gift giver.

People usually put themselves into gift giving. They try to find you just the right thing, something that fits your taste and that you will like. I am usually afraid the look on my face will not say thank-you the way I want it to, or will not make them feel they chose well when they picked my gift. Of course, none of this counts when it pertains to my husband. Spouses just need to come through at Christmas. You live with us all year. Do you honestly want to sit there and say you could not think of anything that might make us happy…that you had no ideas? Seriously?

Christmas is not about the stuff for me. It is about moments. Take the candlelight service at church. I love Christmas Eve services at church, but I especially enjoy the style of my pastor here in Oregon. He makes Christmas Eve candlelight services about family. We sing many Christmas Carols. We read the Christmas story from Scripture. He also selects a story to read to us. Stories like these highlight the real spirit of Christmas and they touch our hearts.

Children are a big part of our service. There is a lot of noise and the sound of many small voices and baby chatter fill the room. Mix it with candlelight, the smiles on most adult faces, the anticipation visible in the eyes and the squirming of the young ones, and it becomes a magical evening for me.

My favorite Christmas Eve memory is a service where our pianist decided to have her young daughter join her at the piano to sing a Christmas duet. Recalling the six-year-old voice accompanying the soft, mellow tones of her mother makes me misty eyed even now. I am a sucker for small children and family moments like these. That moment brought together the whole of Christmas for me: the story of Christ told through song, the wonder of Christmas expressed through the voice of a child, and the stirring of the soul as only beautiful music can do. It tapped in to my own love for the childish voices that sat beside me that night. It reminded me that these moments are to be cherished. My own children would grow up too quickly. Moments of such joy come sparingly and are to be cherished.

Christmas passes so quickly. You prepare for it for months and wait with great anticipation. You make the food that will force you to spend the first three months of the following year removing it from your waistline. You decorate the house with beautiful ornaments and lights. You invite family and friends over for eggnog and hot apple cider. You even smile at strangers on the street. Schedules are organized around getting together with both sides of the family. Christmas events at school and church crowd your schedule. Then it is over. It is time to take down the decorations and clean up the tree. Just like that, Christmas is done for another year.

Much of my life seems to go this way—in flashes. My daughter was born yesterday and today she is taller than I am. Tomorrow she goes off to college. The next day she gets married and moves out. While those four days may take twenty-five or thirty years to occur, they seem to happen overnight.

A progression of Clint Black songs suggests that I am not the only one to struggle with time. One of his earliest hits was a song called *Killing Time,* but within just a few years, he was following it up with *No Time to Kill,* and later, *Spend My Time.* It is not hard to discover that time is a valuable commodity. Mastering our use of time is one of our greatest keys to a happy and healthy life.

Time management guru Brain Tracy once suggested many people confuse activity with accomplishment.[49] The busier we are the more successful we feel. As a culture we seem willing to exchange time for money, and as Harvard professor Juliet Schor points out, once we do this we compensate for all the times we miss in our children's lives by buying more stuff.[50] Since much of that stuff gets put on credit card and long term loans—once started, the vicious circle of work and spend never ends.

How did we get here? How did we move from a culture that valued Sabbath, a day of rest to worship the Lord and spend with family, to a nation that added more hours to the workweek every decade since the 1960's[51]? How did we, a freethinking nation of individualists, become one of the most overworked nations in the world? How did we so quietly give up the month long vacations of our European counterparts? Whatever happened to lazy Sundays and forty hour work weeks? When did our years begin to fly by so quickly? How did free time in our lives get so far out of control? To the real point, do we care?

I care. I want my life back. For me, it all started with a car. I was 17, and I wanted some money of my own. I had the usual few dollars from birthday and Christmas every year. I made some money doing odd jobs for my Grandmother like painting the shed and garage. But that did not add up enough to buy a few pairs of my favorite jeans, to go backpacking in the Adirondacks, or to catch a concert now and then. For those things I needed a real job. I made the rounds of the local stores, and filled out applications for an entry-level position. In a few weeks, I was working as a cashier at a chain grocery store.

It did not take long for me to discover I needed a car. Waiting for Mom's taxi or my brother to drive me got old quickly for all of us. Dad and I went in search of wheels. I became the proud owner of a 1969 Ford Falcon. She was a thing of beauty to no one: two doors, an ugly shade of green and old when I bought her. She was all mine though. Dad and mine's actually. He agreed to loan me the money as long as I agreed to make monthly payments.

That was the beginning of my close association with an ever-increasing car payment. Overnight, I went from wanting a job to make some money for the odd purchase here and there, to needing a job to make car payments. The fun of checking out customers in the grocery store stopped quickly and turned into work. It was also the end of my free time. The connection was now built between work and buying things I wanted. I discovered a few more hours would buy a few more things and I never looked back. At one point I had three jobs, earning a bunch of extra cash, and have never seemed to break the pattern. Though mostly working just one job for the past twenty years, I work between 60-75 hours most weeks.

Why do I do it? I am burned out. I am tired most of the time. I spend far less time with my family than I want. Why am I so stuck in a pattern of work that I have joined the ranks of those who no longer know what to do with a quiet Sunday afternoon? I cannot wait my turn around the traffic circle picking my kids up at the high school without muttering impatiently at the drivers ahead of me—so much so that some of my friends refuse to ride with me anymore. Every day of my date book seems to have ink on it. I cannot see any end in sight.

I do not want a car payment any more. Most days I do not even want a car, but there seem to be a lot of them in my driveway.

I became wedded to my job in order to pay for my stuff, and I cannot see my way out. My husband and I created a way of life that we thought we wanted. Most days we are happy with it. But the truth is this; I no longer run my life. My life runs me. That bumper sticker *I owe, I owe, it's off to work I go* is not funny anymore. I set my sights on a certain standard of living, and now that standard takes its toll on my time. It owns me. I have decided I want to be home more, I just cannot figure out how. Still, I have remembered a wise saying: *To get out of a hole, the first thing to do is stop digging.* I am almost ready to stop digging. Maybe others are also ready to drop their shovels.

As we have bought more, we have started working more. It is as simple as that. It seems time and happiness hold a strong relationship. According to a Harris Research poll, since 1973, free time has fallen nearly 40%, from a median figure of 26 hours to slightly under 17 hours per week.[52] We know this do we not, that when we master our schedules, take control of our lives and spend our time in the ways we choose to, our sense of happiness and well-being increase? As we find more time for the things we enjoy, our stress levels decrease and our physical health improves. For most of us, though, it starts with shopping less, spending less, and simplifying our lives.

This brings us back to God. What was God's plan for how we would spend our time? Personally, I think it says something about God. God started us out naked in the Garden of Eden and not Macy's Department Store. I do not think God created us with an overwhelming urge to accumulate so that we would then spend all our time earning some form of capital to acquire everything we wanted. I think the images of a garden are more in keeping with what the Lord intends.

I cannot take any credit for it since most of my garden memories are bad ones involving an acre of plowed ground and way too many vegetable plants to weed around, but I have a beautiful back yard. My husband created a space where when you step out onto our patio, you can feel tension leave your body. There is a gentle stream flowing down from the back corner into two decorative ponds. Usually there will be a bird or two bathing themselves somewhere along the path. Squirrels jump from tree to fence, in their never-ending quest to find a new way to defeat the squirrel proof bird feeder. An aviary filled with half a dozen cooing doves is near the back gate. It is a peaceful place. I go there whenever I can.

I think God had places like this in mind. God wants us to live in such a way that there is time to wander through gardens, and time to enjoy birds and trees and critters. In our haste to know everything and to possess all the world offers we have thrown away what makes us happy; time to wander among and appreciate things of beauty. God created a beautiful world. I think we were meant to have time to enjoy being part of it.

Dear friends, God is good. So I beg you to offer your bodies to him as a living sacrifice, pure and pleasing. That's the most sensible way to serve God. Don't be like the people of this world, but let God change the way you think. Then you will know how to do everything that is good and pleasing to him. (Romans 12:1,2 CEV)

Let God change the way you think. Be transformed. If I really hate my full schedule, and my date book covered with ink, I have no one to blame but myself. I am the one that writes things into every one of those little squares that make up a month. I am the one who made the decisions to live a style of life that requires massive amounts of our family's time to maintain. I am the one who chose to live at a frantic pace, with little room for time to sit in my garden or read a book. I am the driven one.

But I want to be a Romans 12 person. I want to slow down, to smell flowers in my back yard, and to be fully acquainted with my daughters before they leave home for their journeys in the world. I want to sit on the back patio and enjoy a cup of coffee with my husband as we watch the hummingbirds zip from one feeder to the next, and the jays chase away the wild canaries. I want my life back. I want to own my time again. I want Christmas to linger this year.

Questions for further reflection:
1. What choices have you made that contribute to your own loss of control over time?
2. Read Ecclesiastes 3:1-22 and Psalms 119:1-40. What do you hear God saying to you?
3. Can you envision ways to recapture time? Is it important enough that you would take steps to make those changes?
4. Do you believe we live the way God has in mind for us? What affect does our culture's lifestyle have on the rest of God's creation?

Action Plan
- Make a seven-day calendar showing how you use blocks of time. (Example: Monday morning and afternoon blocks might be labeled "work", and evening block labeled "dinner, choir practice and Monday Night Football") Begin noting the patterns. Look for places you would like to make changes.
- Now make a wish calendar. Do it as if money was not an issue and you could work fewer hours. Make this calendar your goal as you move to the next step. No plan—little hope of success! If you want to see your children or spouse more – start blocking them in. If you want to find time for tea with a friend, get rid of something that keeps you from doing that. Do you want to spend 5 p.m. on the patio every night with your spouse? Plan for it.

- Now make a six-month calendar that feels better. Make only small adjustments in this one, knowing that change takes time, and adjustments made slowly have more potential for actually turning into permanent changes. Perhaps it is time to let go of a club or organization. Maybe a job needs to be curbed, or a volunteer role should be scaled down. Maybe Saturday morning shopping could be moved to an evening—forcing you to shop more quickly and make fewer impulse buys.
- Find two other people who are overworked, tired of their schedule, and overwhelmed by the busy-ness of their lives. Meet together to share your goals and to hold one another accountable. We are often far more successful at achieving goals when we are held accountable by friends. Find ways to meet without adding stress to the schedule. Perhaps you could walk together and simultaneously meet your exercise goals; or you could regularly discuss this during play dates for your kids.

If you want to know more:
- Juliet Schor, *The Overworked American*
- Wayne Muller, Sabbath: *Restoring the Sacred Rhythm of Rest*
- Brian Tracy, *Eat That Frog*
- Steve Ganger, *Time Warped*

Swimming Upstream

"I realized I was always tired," my friend Steve told me. "I was always working. Even during the evening and on days at home with my family I took calls and answered e-mail. There was never a time I felt like I could relax. It beat me down. All that changed for me when I started reading about Sabbath time.

"A year ago I began to take a full day off each week. Starting the evening before, I shut off my computer and cell phone and put away all my deskwork. Then for thirty-eight hours, I relax and enjoy my family. I sleep late and read the news slowly over morning coffee. I putter in the garden and take walks with my wife or ride bike with my kids. During each Sabbath, I set aside time to sit and enjoy God's creation. I leave time for solitude and let the Lord speak to me.

"As Sabbath became a pattern in my life my energy level slowly returned. I enjoyed life more. It was as if my body and soul were telling me they needed time to restore. It amazes me that a focused time of rest and relaxation does so much for my attitude and peace of mind."

Holidays or Holy Days
Making it harder to swim against the current

From a commercial point of view, if Christmas did not exist it would be necessary to invent it.

Katharine Whitehorn

Oh look, yet another Christmas TV special! How touching to have the meaning of Christmas brought to us by cola, fast food, and beer.... Who'd have ever guessed that product consumption, popular entertainment, and spirituality would mix so harmoniously?

Bill Watterson, Calvin & Hobbes

Halloween now gobbles up $2.5 billion in candy, soft drinks, costumes, decorations and beer.

Juliet Schor

I hate Christmas. I know I will spend money I do not have on gifts that people do not need, and work more hours the next six months to pay for them. Next to the gifts my brother will bring, mine will look weak for one more year. Why not just hang out together and eat Grandma's cookies?

A single Mom

I started my professional life as a history teacher. I loved teaching so it came as a surprise to spend such a short time doing it. While I feel like I am where God wants me—working in camp ministry—I enjoyed the teaching profession.

Teaching increased my love for holidays. Everyone thinks it is the schoolchildren who look forward to extra days off. They forget what it is like to keep children cooped up for seven hours on a beautiful fall day! Despite turning all the desks in the opposite direction of the windows, convincing young minds that they had any vested interest in learning about Christopher Columbus or Ponce de Leon was just plain rough going even on a rainy day. It became impossible on a beautiful fall one. I took to bringing cookies and juice on the days I was teaching about the early explorers. Bribery seemed the only workable approach.

That is what made holidays so cool. If tigers were allowed to roam free an extra day a week, they felt less caged during school the other four. It was good for them and a breather for me. I worked most Saturdays correcting homework and putting lessons together, so it was nice to get a break. I came to love Christmas and Easter, Columbus Day and Thanksgiving more deeply. I had difficulty remembering my younger brother's birthday, but I could tell you when George Washington's was!

That was my old life. In my new life that came after teaching, I now have second thoughts about holidays. Holidays have slipped from days of getting extra rest and having special times with family to opportunities for marketers to make a large profit from my wallet.

I am writing this the day after Columbus Day. I am as excited about North America as the next person, and am glad Christopher Columbus established a connection between the hemispheres, but does a celebration of this event really require an extra twelve flyers in the newspaper, all telling me about their blow-out Columbus Day sale? Is every holiday meant to be about buying stuff?

The word holiday was originally the contraction of the two words holy and day. Holy is seldom seen in holidays any more. Instead, holidays are opportunities for us to shop. While we all know about Christmas shopping, Easter has also entered the massive consumerism game.

I asked my Mom once what Easter looked like for her as a child growing up after the Great Depression. She remembered receiving one new thing for church—a pair of shoes, a blouse or dress, and an Easter Basket with a chocolate bunny, some marshmallow chicks and a few jelly beans. The day centered on church and a family dinner.

When I was a child in the 1960's Easter had expanded. Easter meant not only a basket filled the best chocolate I would see all year; it also included a new dress to wear to church. For much of the first decade of their lives, I followed those traditions with my daughters. There were nice dresses and Easter hats, and always a great Easter basket filled with candy.

Easter kept ratcheting up for me. My girls had Grandparents, aunts and uncles who spoiled them terribly. Not only did they get cool Easter stuff from their Dad and me—they could also count on an Easter gift from their extended family. Where I could count on an Easter basket from Mom and Dad, my kids were brought up believing it is normal to receive something from just about the whole family. Easter for them is a lot like Christmas, only with more chocolate.

This is where Easter took another twist in my family. Extended family members who were part of the celebration, but who wanted to limit how much sugar a child should have, began placing plastic eggs filled with money or stuff in the Easter baskets instead of candy. Easter shifted from a time of coloring eggs and waking up to find them in the basket to one more day marked by spending and getting.

This contrast between holy day and holiday could not be more striking. A day when Christians the world over rise before dawn to gather together and worship the risen Lord—the holiest of all holy days—now provides a day for Americans to spend billions of dollars on Easter-related consumer goods. Retail insiders tell us *"Easter is gaining relevance as a retail holiday."*[53] Christ now competes with the Easter bunny in many homes on Easter morning. In too many homes the bunny is winning.

Christmas leaves a starker picture. Can we blame it on the Wise Men? Had they not brought gifts to the Christ child, none of this would have happened! They started it more or less (Smile please. I am joking!). As much as 50% of all sales in the average retail store can happen during the Christmas buying season[54]. Sometimes it feels like that 25% is occurring in my family alone! I am not joking anymore.

When I was a child, my Dad was a truck driver for the local milk plant. Christmas did not start for us until Dad got home, and Dad did not get home until the cows were milked. As a five or six year old, it felt like every cow in the state of New York had to be milked first. As a result, Christmas gift giving in our home took place mid-afternoon.

In my childhood home, exchanging gifts meant I received eight to ten packages under the tree from my parents. Later on Christmas day, we would make our way to one of my Grandparents' homes. There we would receive one more gift. On another weekend during the Christmas season we would head to the other set of Grandparents for a final gift. These ten to twelve gifts, time with Mom and Dad and my Grandparents made me think Christmas was the coolest time of year!

I have great Christmas memories but few are of a particular gift. My memories center on family members and feelings of belonging, the deserts my Grandmothers were famous for, my Aunt Jeannine's escalloped oysters, and the Christmas where Grandpa started pretending the dinner rolls were baseballs and pitched them to my cousin.

Fast forward to today. My children grew up with mountains of presents under the tree at every house in our extended family. Each year the price tag for the festivities just goes up. When they were young, my daughters received some cute stuffed animals, children's books and a store's worth of child's toys and games. Now they get bicycles and iPods, coffee cards and gift certificates to their favorite stores. One trendy shirt alone costs more than everything I would have found under the tree. Now the trendy shirt is just one of dozens of gifts.

We are the ones to blame. Dad and Mom. We do not ask other family members to tone it down, and we do not set limits.

How did we get here? How did days once marked by family and tradition, become Hallmark moments? How did we move from a time where a few presents under the tree seemed like a big deal to one where opening less than a dozen gifts seems like an off year? Is it good for us to be doing this?

For me, the answer is no. I notice that Christmas is one of the most stressful moments in the year. There is too much to do and it adds too many bills to my expenses. It is too easy to spend more than I have. The part that grieves me the most is that I am sending wrong messages to my kids. I created a Christmas season that is about shopping malls and getting cool stuff at the expense of everything Christmas represents.

My Mother, and her Mother before her, describe Christmas differently. Christmas began months in advance with decisions about what gifts would be under the tree for the youngsters. Since some gifts would be hand-made, advance planning was important. Sewing and crocheting began in earnest, and Christmas lists would be inspected for one or two items chosen by the children from the J.C. Penny's and Sears catalogues.

Baking began the first week of December. Batches of cookies would be made, and then frozen so everyone could have their favorites during the holiday season. Sugar cookies were among the most popular, because we loved to frost them and then dump sprinkles and candies on top. Pies and fudge came last to keep them fresh. These baking projects were a family affair. Friends helped too. Kids were everywhere. Stories were shared and memories of earlier Christmases revisited. Pot after pot of tea and hot chocolate were made and then used for dunking anything that could remotely be labeled a misfit.

When several kinds of cookies were ready, we put trays together for folks we knew could not make cookies of their own. I remember knocking on the front doors of several grandfather types from church who had lost their spouses, and women whose arthritis prevented them from baking much anymore. We gave them trays of cookies decorated with red bows and a little glitter.

Christmas was three weeks worth of evenings and weekends spent baking, making presents to give away, and laughing and sharing with family and friends. One day in there somewhere was a family trip to the closest department stores, usually a weeknight early in the month because Dad hated waiting in line. It was our one shopping trip. We went with a list of whom we needed to shop for; bought them the one gift we were going to buy and we were done. It took one night.

I contrast my childhood shopping experiences to my one and only experience with the Friday after Thanksgiving shopping frenzy. My girls were little, we were broke, and I discovered that the early shopper specials included free stuff if you were among the first one hundred in the door. I parked in front of the store at 5:45 a.m., only to discover that to be one of the first one hundred in the store meant pushing my way past several dozen people, most of who looked grumpier than I did. I concluded stores could really improve things on the biggest shopping day of the year if they would hand out some free coffee in their cold, dark parking lots. They want us to drag ourselves out of bed at an ungodly hour to buy their stuff. If they would put a cup of coffee in our hands they would be amazed how much more Christmas cheer we customers could scrape up at that hour of the morning. Just a thought!

The day after Thanksgiving is no longer the start of shopping. Many of us start shopping after Halloween and end it on the way to Grandma's on Christmas Eve. One big family trip to the department store has been replaced by a month of trips to the mall, outlet stores, and specialty shops. When all that fails, we make last minute purchases online with expensive overnight delivery, or head off to 7-11.

Why have we allowed days that were about family, friends, and relationship building to be traded for shopping and gift giving?

Why, when we repeatedly say we do not get enough time with our families, do we use the time we do have at a mall instead of making popcorn, watching *Rudolph* or *White Christmas,* or playing card or board games with our children? Do we honestly think the best thing we can do for our children, our parents, our friends and our extended family is to buy them something? Do we really think the best way to show our family we love them is to come through the Christmas season with a stack of credit card slips? No wonder depression and suicide rates rise at Christmas!

Whether birthdays, Christmas, Easter or Mother's Day, our holiday behavior says a lot about our culture and what we value. To this day, one of my favorite birthdays was one I spent with my Uncle, eating dinner at one of our town's nicer restaurants. We shared the same birthday, and I asked him to celebrate it with me that year. Not a present in sight, but time shared with a person who mattered to me instead. Yet these days, I usually find myself buying a gift card to some store or restaurant last minute, and rarely spend any serious time with the recipient of the gift.

My holiday behavior does not say the right things about my values anymore. As I finish writing this chapter I have returned from a birthday party for a person I met through work and who became my friend. He has few needs and expected no gifts, but I found it virtually impossible to arrive empty handed. I had a war with myself even as I was driving there. I finally discovered a compromise. I stopped at the drugstore at the edge of town and bought him a small birthday bag full of Hershey Hugs and Kisses. Maybe it was an early step for me in going against the flow....

Questions for further reflection:
1. Why do you think we have become a culture that has turned every holiday and special event into a gift exchange?
2. Describe your favorite holiday memory. What made it special?

3. Does spending for holidays and family birthdays ever put a strain on your finances? Do you feel good about the expenses?
4. Think about someone you love. What would you most like to receive from them on your next birthday? What about that gift makes it important to you?

Action Plan:
- Gift giving has become a significant expense for us. Consider holding a family council, and discussing this chapter. If your family is like mine, you struggle to find something others want or need, frequently ending up with impersonal gift certificates to a favorite store. Are there things you would rather do as a family than exchange gift cards? Are there places you might celebrate together? Could you rent a cabin for a weekend or spend days picnicking at the lake? Talk with your family about what you would like your children to remember when they grow up. Begin planning to make that possible.
- Find ways to invest time in each other on special days and holidays. Here is an example: instead of an expensive gift, take your child to the park and play catch, or to a budget movie and talk about it afterwards over hot chocolate. Go fishing with your brother or take dessert to your Mom's house and play her favorite game. Do something that involves your heart and minimizes your expense.
- Be the person in your circle to focus on spending time with loved ones on holidays, not spending money. Someone has to start. Let it be you.

If you want to know more:
- Purchase a book such as *Christmas Gifts of Good Taste* (Leisure Arts, 1991) and discover ways to make gift giving personal.
- Get in touch with your family's oral history. Ask a parent or grandparent to share their favorite memories of what a holiday looked like to them as a child.

Swimming Upstream

"Last year at Christmas our office decided to do something different for our annual gift exchange. Instead of getting the usual small presents for one another, we decided to pick a mission project and give the money we would normally have spent to that project. There are only five of us so it was not a large amount, about $125. We felt great about it though. Instead of purchasing things none of us needed, we bought bedding and small stuffed animals for a shelter for abused women and children. Our donation made a difference for several families who needed help.

"During the time we would normally do this gift exchange we went around a circle sharing a story of how we were blessed by someone else during the past year. It was the best office Christmas party ever."

Dead Fish Everywhere
Climate Change and Wasted Fish

Thank God men cannot fly, and lay waste the sky as well as the earth.

Henry David Thoreau

There's so much pollution in the air now that if it weren't for our lungs there'd be no place to put it all.

Robert Orben

We do not inherit the earth from our ancestors, we borrow it from our children.

Native American Proverb

Oh Beautiful for smoggy skies, insecticided grain, For strip-mined mountain's majesty above the asphalt plain.
America, America, man sheds his waste on thee, And hides the pines with billboard signs, from sea to oily sea.

George Carlin

When we heal the earth, we heal ourselves.

David Orr

The activist is not the man who says the river is dirty. The activist is the man who cleans up the river.

Ross Perot

When one tugs at a single thing in nature, he finds it attached to the rest of the world.

John Muir

The debate drags on. Is global warming a reality, or just the product of faulty science and incomplete studies? I will acknowledge my bias up front. I believe it is relevant that not a single major scientific study reviewed by a group of peers challenges global warming. Whether you believe in climate change or not is beside the point. The real question to ask is of an entirely different nature. Are we living our lives and caring for all that God has given us in a God honoring way? In other words, are we good stewards? Do we do a good job of managing the earth?

I hate house cleaning. I do not mean the weekly dusting and vacuuming, though I am not fond of that either. I mean the all out cleaning where the unwanted, unneeded and unused stuff moves from my house to somewhere else. I hate going through closets and cupboards. I hate going through the attic and the garage. I grew up with depression era parents who believed that if you got rid of it today you were going to need it tomorrow, so my idea of cleaning is to move stuff from the house to the next open space in the garage, attic or shed. Then one avoids those places in the future.

Unfortunately for me, I married a man raised by post depression parents. When he says clean, it does not mean shuffling stuff from one place to the next. This difference caused uncounted arguments the first decade of our married life. Now I am too busy arguing with my teenage daughters to have the energy to argue with my husband about housecleaning.

Our difference in backgrounds means we each needed to give a little. My husband allows far more to be kept in the garage than he would like, and I say goodbye to a much larger percentage of stuff than I ever would have imagined. It works for us. Where the rubber hits the road is in our yearly house cleaning. About twice a year he reaches a *that is the last time I am walking around all this junk* state of mind and my day is over until the house is clean. If I work strategically, I can minimize the chore to whatever room brought on the declaration—the garage, our walk-in closet or the coat closet downstairs. When I did not work strategically, we tackle all three. Those are not friendly days, and I do not recommend them for the faint of heart or the newly married.

Even after a few hours of sorting, piles remain. There will be a Salvation Army pile with all the clothes that no longer fit, or are deemed by my children as too outdated or boring to wear, and all the used appliances and electronics we could not live without and now cannot live with. There will be a recycling pile and a returnable pile with all the stuff that can be taken back for a deposit or recycled for reuse. Then there is the dump pile where we put the things that do not apply to the other piles. That stuff is thrown away.

I discovered that if I agree to take stuff to the Salvation Army and recycling center I could avoid the last hour of the incredible drudgery that is housecleaning. I get rid of the other junk and my husband does the final trash run, sweeping and clean up. Again, it works for us. Although, now that I wrote this down I am not sure how much longer I can get away with my strategy of not helping to finish the job.

As I haul away the still-in-good-shape category of stuff, I recognize the magnitude of the issue. I have yet to pull up in front of a second hand store without seeing mountains of stuff waiting to be sorted out. Not only are the store shelves packed full of everything including the kitchen sink, but the drop off point outside the store is filled to overflowing. My leftovers are added to the tons of everybody else's leftovers.

Despite your beliefs about the temperature of the earth and any human role in it, can you imagine that God is okay with one culture having so much that it routinely carts millions of tons of things to a second hand store while dozens of other cultures have so little they can stack everything they own on a small blanket under the eaves of a city storefront? Does God mind that we destroy the beauty of Alaska in order to remove every drop of oil to power our way of life; or that litter lines our highways, lakes and streams? Is it all right with the Lord that a layer of grey blocks the sky over our cities, or that artificial light makes it increasingly difficult to see the majesty of the star-filled night? I believe the answer is no. God is probably not too keen on our earth management skills.

We might need some re-training. If we are trying to become counter-cultural fishes swimming upstream, it might be time to note that dead fish are everywhere.

In college I was required to write a paper on some aspect of ecology for an education class. It was the 1970's with *Mother Earth News* becoming a noted publication and environmental issues hitting the national stage. I chose the topic of recycling. Through my research I discovered that Oregon was the only state at the time with a bottle bill requiring drink cans to carry a deposit. Though some other states were working on similar bills and others encouraged the collection of aluminum for recycling, no one else put the same effort into it as Oregon.

Now that I live here, I am proud of Oregon and what it does to protect the environment. Though the balance is often a painful dance between loggers and environmentalists—developers and preservationists, I want it no other way. With that in mind, it is heartbreaking to see my state still having one of the most polluted rivers flowing through the heart of our population.

A 2000 L.A. Times article claimed *"The Willamette River, whose citizen-led cleanup in the 1960s inspired the nation to reclaim its waterways, has become so tainted by sewage and industrial waste that it faces being listed as a federal Superfund site—the roster of the country's most polluted places,"*[55] Oregon, a state that takes pride in its environmental record, finds controlling pollution and caring for the earth a chore.

Few of us have focused on environmental issues like these as Christian issues. Some churches even take the stance that since God is coming back to take us home, it does not matter what we do to the earth. Other churches preach a message that God gave us this earth for our own pleasure so it is ours to treat as we wish.

Pope John Paul II held that "Modern Society will find no solution to the ecological problem unless it takes a serious look at its lifestyles[56]." I am with the Pope on this one, but I would add one more piece to the mix. Until we first believe that caring for creation is a religious issue, and until we acknowledge that our lifestyles have a direct impact on creation, there will not be solutions anytime soon.

I had an acquaintance who owned several homes, renting them out as investment properties. His goal was to buy up multiple houses and use the rental income they produced as his retirement income. His idea was better in theory than in practice. He grossly underestimated what could go wrong. Since rent money was the money he used to pay the mortgages and to live on, it did not take long for trouble to hit.

His intention was to save money by doing any repair work himself. However, his plan was also to spend his winters in Florida.

When the roof needed fixing in January he called a local carpenter to do the work. That would have been fine except for the series of repairs that followed in close succession. A water heater gave up the ghost. A window got shattered in one house. The furnace quit in another. The renters moved out in a third with no new prospects in sight.

This dragged on for years. The money never quite came in at the rate it was anticipated. The upkeep bills exceeded advanced planning. The result was a series of rundown homes that no longer fit in the neighborhood. He had become a slumlord, an owner that invested little in the property while at the same time pulling every conceivable piece of income back out.

I would suggest to you that we might be the same. As long as we ignore earth care we remain property owners of an increasingly shabby property who drain the value from the asset, not keeping it in good repair for the use of others.

To borrow an idea from Tom Peters[57], those things we pay attention to we accomplish. I spent a lot of time reading about consumerism, stewardship and financial health during my Doctoral Studies. Several of the books brought on the same aha moments for me. I am a little sad to say this because the premise of these books was all too simplistic. Since these books were big sellers, I take comfort in not being the only one slow to get the point.

David Bach's *The Automatic Millionaire* is a great example[58]. He says you must pay attention to the habit of saving or some form of investing. If you do not focus your savings effort, your savings will not accumulate. As Bach correctly points out, if you would focus on savings long enough to put an automatic monthly withdrawal in place and then you leave it alone for a long period, you are going to accumulate with minimal effort.

Rocket science this is not. It simply illustrates what happens if you focus. If creating a savings account or investment portfolio is important to me, I must develop and act on a plan in a disciplined way.

Caring for the earth falls into the same category. I think God means for us to take care of what was created for us. I am reminded of a beautiful cutting board my grandfather made for me. I had a hard time using it, not just because it was beautiful, but also because it brought back memories of Grandpa. This was a mistake. Grandpa wanted me to use it. He wanted me to enjoy the beauty of the wood he had chosen, and he wanted me to remember him and the great relationship we had.

I think God might be a little like Grandpa and the cutting board. God made the earth for us and wants us to enjoy it. I just think maybe there is divine disappointment in our effort of caring for creation. Like Pope John Paul, I believe nothing will change until we change our lifestyle. Like Tom Peters, I think focus will be the key to the solution.

I already wrote about my love of water. Water always reminds me of God. If I want those lakes, rivers and oceans that have been food for my soul to remain sources of beauty for my grandchildren, it is time I pay attention.

"The earth is the Lord's and everything in it," the Psalmist tells us (Psalm 24). We have paid scant attention to the implications of the Psalmist's words. I believe I am a lousy tenant *and* a lousy property owner. It is time for me to be transformed, and for me to get concerned about creation. I need to start swimming upstream.

Questions for further reflection:

1. What do you believe about global climate change? How and why do you believe this?
2. What do you think God expects from us when it comes to the earth? How does Scripture inform your belief?
3. Does your church talk about caring for God's creation? If no, why do you think that is? Do you believe the church should talk about these issues?
4. In what ways does your lifestyle demonstrate your care for creation?
5. Is your lifestyle an adequate reflection of how you believe God wants you to manage all that was made?

Action Plan

- Read a chapter or two from one of the books listed at the end of this chapter. Take some time to spend with God in reflection. What do you hear God saying to you?

- Make creation care a topic of your congregation's prayers. If we want to have a significant impact in managing the earth and its critters, what better place to focus on it than through our life together in prayer?
- Organize a cleanup crew. Choose a stretch of highway, a park or an area in your community that needs care. Publicize your efforts! Though the Bible shares that it is good to do good deeds in secret, in the area of caring for creation, the world needs to see Christ's church leading the way. If the church does not show proper concern for all that God has made, who will?
- Resolve to be a part of the solution to the earth's health problems. Contribute less to waste and recycling. Consider buying local products to save energy resources. Buy goods when they are in season locally and help save the energy used by transporting them from far away.

If you want to know more
- www.flylady.com
- www.epa.gov
- www.mennocreationcare.org
- Google "environmental websites" and "creation care" to find a couple of websites that speak to you. Learn as much as you can about creation care.
- Read Bill McKibben, *The End of Nature*
- Read Lester Brown, *Plan B 2.0*. The best look at the effect of humanity on the planet, though it is initially overwhelming. It is worth reading to the end, as Brown offers solutions once he gets beyond painting the picture of just how bad the problem is.
- Read Fred Pearce, *When the Rivers Runs Dry*
- Read Stephen Bouma-Prediger, *For the Beauty of the Earth*. Though not a quick read, this book provides a solid Biblical foundation for the subject.
- Read Henry David Thoreau, *Walden*
- Read any story by Wendell Berry. Berry has such a love for nature and an easy way of sharing. His depictions of a simpler way of life provide food for the soul.

Swimming Upstream

"It has only been the last year or two that I gave this any thought," Jennifer told me. "As gas prices went up I started paying more attention. It cost a lot of money to bring fresh vegetables to Oregon in January. They have to be trucked or flown to Oregon from farms in California or South America. By the time they do this, two things have happened: the cost has gone up in order to pay for the transportation and natural resources are used to get that product here for me to buy. I never paid any attention before. If I wanted fresh strawberries in January I just bought them."

"Now that I started paying attention I decided to shop differently. Instead of purchasing from the chain grocery store, I now make the effort to buy as much local produce as I can. I go to my favorite farm stand and I stock up on what is in season. Even when the farm stand closes for the winter, I try to buy locally produced products that did not require using an abundance of natural resources in getting them to me. I envy the folks who have time to can or freeze local fruits and vegetables, but I personally do not have the time to do it myself. I can, however, pay attention to what I buy and try to shop with an eye to what is good for the local economy and the environment. I believe that if we all made just a few small changes, we could have a dramatic impact on the amount of natural resources we use as a nation. Buy local! Help a local farmer and save natural resources!"

Happy to be a Guppy,
Even in a School of Angelfish
Waving goodbye to the Jones family

The secret weapon of environmental change and of
social justice must be this – living with simple elegance
is more pleasurable than living caught in the middle of
our consumer culture.
                    Bill McKibbon Comforting Whirlwind

I make myself rich by making my wants few.
                    Henry David Thoreau

I would like to live like the Jones family. I must admit it. It
would be fun to drive their Lexus, take a vacation to the Bahamas,
and send my kids off to Dartmouth or Yale. The reality for me,
however, is what I like to do for a living does not place me in the
same income bracket as the Jones family. When I pretend I am a
Jones I just end up in debt. I try spending as they do and slap my
Visa gold down on the counter. Then the bill shows up and I realize I am not a Jones after all.

Study after study and interview after interview have taught us
a few things. First, we like being the big fish in a little pond. Americans admit they are happier when they know they are making more
than their neighbors are. As bizarre as it seems, we report that we
are happier making $50,000 when our neighbors are making
$40,000, than if we were making $60,000 but our neighbors all
made $70,000[59]. We find it hard to feel good being a guppy when
we are surrounded by a neighborhood full of angelfish.

Second, the more stuff we buy for ourselves the less likely we
are to let our money support our community.[60] I will never forget
The Meanness Mania[61], the title of one of my Political Science
texts. When my professor described the 1960's and 1970's, he discussed his observation of a growing state of selfishness—an overwhelming cult of meanness—taking over society. Basically put, as

I discover what money can do for me I become less concerned about building roads and repairing bridges, improving schools and paying for top notch teachers, funding Head Start programs and providing services for an ever increasing pool of elderly folks living at the poverty level.[62] In fact, as we get more caught up in consumerism, a case can be built that we are becoming less willing to extend even the most common of courtesies—holding the door open for the person with their hands full or slowing down to allow a few cars to turn into the school drop off lane ahead of us. Consumerism has even affected our manners.

Third, even though we own more stuff and have more opportunities at our fingertips than any generation before us, we still feel we are poorer than those we followed.[63] The more we get, the more we seem to need that we do not yet have. Children have long lists of the things they want to buy. However, once those things are attained the appeal wears off quickly.

Finally, although we claim our nation is too materialistic, and agree that others try to keep up with the Jones family, we falsely believe those other people do not influence our thinking[64]. However, our actions betray these beliefs. Nearly half of all car owners saw their car as a reflection of who they are, either a lot or some.[65] Some confess they cannot stomach the thought of having a Taurus parked in the driveway when their neighbors drive a Volvo, Lexus or BMW.[66]

Financial analysts have long said the beginning of our financial pressures begin with the purchase of a car. I can only shake my head in wonder. Maybe it is time for me to stop trying to be like the Jones family—you know, the big fish in the pond—and to happily live like the guppy I am.

Consider what life in the slower, simpler, happier lane could look like. You would have a smaller house, but one paid off in time to retire earlier and live the way you want to live. You might have an older car, driven for more years, but money in savings that enables you to take family vacations paid for by cash. You would not buy as many frivolous, time-wasting items, but would have enough cash to have a financial buffer against tragedy or financial reversal. The slow lane means fewer gadgets in your home, but cupboards and closets in which you can find what you seek. You would have more time to spend with family and friends because you will not need to work those extra hours paying off five credit cards.

So why are more of us failing to say goodbye to the Jones family? Family downsizing works for those who try it. My brother provides a great example. When he and his wife started life together, they earned good salaries as two income professionals. As they began preparing for children, they increased their savings for a stronger financial cushion. My sister-in-law switched to part-time work in order to stay home with the kids after they were born. Their money was tighter but they adjusted their spending, bought a used car instead of new, ate at home more often and visited Starbucks less.

When a job opportunity arose for my sister-in-law, they decided to become a single income family, and now my brother stays home with my niece and nephew. Once both kids are in school he will return to the work force and begin rebuilding the savings account they drew from in order to raise their family in the way they wanted.

In the meantime, he has a life many Dads dream about—running around the back yard with his son and building art projects with his daughter. He does not enjoy diapers. Who does? Still, it is a life he loves. This life began with their choices and planning ways to make that life possible. They were willing to downsize and had the intestinal fortitude to stop buying stuff. They determined what was important to them, weighing what would be lost and what would be gained, and then made the necessary sacrifices to lead the life they wanted.

Saying goodbye to the Jones family may be one of the hardest things we do, and one of the most important decisions we make. A business consultant once told me that his couch looked old. Yet, more important than earning money for a new couch was preserving the time he set aside to spend with his young sons. Given the choice between money and family, he chose family.

Another colleague of mine gives credit to his wife for raising their children well. He freely admits he was rarely there personally.

Two choices. Two routes. One chose to be there personally as much as possible, and the other chose to work harder so that his wife did not need to be employed and could stay home herself. Both gave up new cars and splashy vacations in exchange for the lifestyle they chose, and both express few regrets.

As for me, I am still trying to get comfortable with owning a dumpy couch—the one that allows me to work less and sit on it more.

My memories of sociology class include stories of immigrant families who came to this country searching for a better life for themselves and their children. Their focus was on the generations that would follow them. They worked hard and often invested immediately in schools, community centers and churches so their children could have a better life. Adults would also be able to gather and care for one another in a community. Self-interest was not all that mattered. Sacrifices were made so that the lives of their children and grandchildren could be better.

These immigrant families sacrificed in the present in order to improve life for their children in the future. Making due with less today means money is available to send the eldest to college tomorrow. Putting things off was simply their way of life. Sure all that stuff in the Sears catalog looked appealing, but few considered buying much beyond essentials. Luxuries were just that—luxuries. Family goals came first. Contrast that to America today where the average credit card debt is now approaching $9,000[67], and pulling equity from homes to finance vacations, cars, and toys has become a national pastime.

How did we get to be a consumer nation when we come from such disciplined immigrant roots? And if we choose to, how do we get back? How do we wave goodbye to the Jones family? The answers are surprisingly simple. It begins with a decision to change, and then becomes a reality through a plan that is acted upon in a consistent way. The tough part is to make that first decision to change one's lifestyle and spending habits.

Personally, I am convinced to make the change. I want a life with fewer work hours and more time to spend with family. I want to sleep stress free, with no worry about credit card debt or how to pay for car repairs. I want less stuff in my house, and less clutter in

my closets, garage and attic. I want to know I planned for retirement in line with my estate goals and in a way that lets me live the
way I want in my senior years.

So, what next? My family began with a family meeting. We
sat down with a list of questions. All four of us listed a dozen things
that make us happy. Next, we wrote down what each of us consider
most important in life. We discovered time and money are the
biggest obstacles to doing more of what we enjoy.

Our family meeting gave us a great opportunity to talk with
our children about how purchasing decisions have such an impact
on doing what we want as a family. Driving the new car our two
kids would like to see us buy means less money to take a trip to
Disney or fly east to see Grandpa and Grandma. Turns out the new
car was not as important as first thought....

Our family conversations continued. We began to stack items
up against one another. What mattered more—a stainless steel
refrigerator with an icemaker in the door, or a trip to New York at
Christmas? Should mom be at home to share more dinners and
play more Scrabble, or should mom work more hours to pay for a
big screen TV or karate lessons? Comparing our preferences
against what we determined was important to us showed us that our
material stuff did not rank as high as we once thought.

Next, we made lists of ten ways each of us thought we could
save money. Even after subtracting ideas like selling a sibling, we
found we had some good places to start. We made a pledge to go to
the store with a list and not deviate from it. Since shopping malls
provide so much temptation, we agreed to limit our trips to the mall
to once a month, and to go with specific needs in mind rather than
to view it as a form of entertainment.

The most important thing we did was to look at our total
financial picture. This helped our kids and us to understand where
we were spending money and why. Enabling them to see what
mortgage payments, electric bills, cable TV and insurance payments do to paychecks helped them put family spending in perspective. Adding savings for emergencies, vacations and retirement
to this list of expenses reduced their ability to eat out, go away for
the weekend, and blow money when shopping.

Our attempts at cutting back have had mixed results. I cannot
get over my whining about a sunroom. My daughters still hope to

go to Hawaii. Some trips to the mall were more successful at restraint than others. Some purchases still make me ask myself, "why?" a day or two later. Overall though, we are developing patterns that will have a long term, positive impact. My children might want just as many things, but they are more realistic in what fits with our plan. Getting stuff is no longer as important as time doing things our family enjoys. Bike riding together has become as much fun as a spin around the mall. Delayed gratification is slowly making its presence known in our household. Our savings account finally exists somewhere other than in our dreams.

The Jones family is going water skiing with their new boat this weekend, and we are not. Their RV is parked under a canopy next to their house, and our tent is on a shelf in the garage. They undoubtedly will have fun with their toys, but I am no longer particularly jealous of them. I will sleep well tonight, and have time to play table games with my daughters before tomorrow evening is gone. Being a Guppy has its moments too.

Action Plan
- Plan a family meeting and educate yourselves about where the money goes. Have each family member make a list of what is most important to him or her and what brings happiness. Is the money spent in ways that help achieve the dreams each of you hold?
- The time to think about tomorrow is today. Unless you feel good about moving into your kid's garage at age sixty-five, (and trust me, they do not feel good about that) now would be a good time to plan for a retirement income. It is not too late—but the time is now. Pull all your information together, and make a plan to build a retirement income. You may have to start small, but start!
- Teach the next generation about managing their finances and planning for the future. Freely discuss money, savings and planning for the future with your children and the children of your church.

If you want to know more
- Dave Ramsey has several excellent books on getting your financial house in order. *The Total Money Makeover* is a great place to start, but any of his books will help build the motivation to begin the planning process.
- Magazines like *Money* or *Forbes* can provide templates of how others have tackled their financial problems, and the msn.com money page often gives great tips. Each of these sources will increase your financial knowledge and help you make better decisions for your financial future. You will be amazed by the number of folks in the same position you are, and encouraged to learn that there are solutions.
- Read David Myers, *The American Paradox*

Swimming Upstream

"Money is such a big deal. I wish someone told me the things I know now. We developed a seminar on just such a wish. A bunch of us got together and made a list of all the things we wish we had known at twenty years of age. Now, one Saturday each fall, we invite all our congregation's young adults and newly married to a pizza party. Several of us share stories about where we went wrong and what we wish we had done differently. Then a woman from our church who works as a bank officer stands up to explain the value of monthly savings and compound interest. It only takes a few examples of how a small amount saved consistently over a long period becomes hundreds of thousands for retirement. They get the picture quickly!

"I spent so many hours worrying about money! If I had just started with a budget when I was young—this much goes to savings, this much for charity, this much for spending—I would not have needed to worry. When a problem came up I would have had the savings to deal with it. When I got ready to retire I could plan to live the lifestyle I wanted instead of working part time to make ends meet. This is why I think it is so important we offer our seminar. It helps our young people get started out right. We also offer individual financial counseling sessions for anyone who is interested. I am so glad someone else can learn from my mistakes!"

The Legacy we Leave our Grandfish
Train up a child

Parents spent 30 hours a week with their children in 1965, and 17 hours in 1985.

David Myers

The easiest way for your children to learn about money is for you not to have any.

Katherine Whitehorn

Teach your children right from wrong, and when they are grown they will still do right.

Proverbs 22:6

In my daughter's eyes I am a hero
I am strong and wise and I know no fear
But the truth is plain to see
She was sent to rescue me
I see who I wanna be
In my daughter's eyes

In my daughter's eyes everyone is equal
Darkness turns to light and the
world is at peace
This miracle God gave to me gives me
strength when I am weak
I find reason to believe
In my daughter's eyes

Martina McBride, In My Daughter's Eyes

I loved the book *Everything I Needed to Know I Learned in Kindergarten*[68]. The title contains a great deal of truth. The more we learn about personality development and how socialization occurs, the more we realize that much of who we are and what we become solidifies at an early age. The wisdom of "train up a child in the way they should go" (Proverbs 22:6) is not mere whimsy.

I spend far less time on training my children than I would like, and I get the distinct feeling I am not alone. The choices I made and the lifestyle I chose determined the amount of time spent with our daughters and the way I helped raise them. I rarely sat down to reflect on what I taught my kids. Now that I am focusing on it, I can only thank God again for God's incredible grace.

The October 2007 issue of *Money* had an article about boomers turning fifty, and the things they plan to do differently in the second half of life. It strikes me with tremendous sadness that one of the top things they plan to do differently is invest more time in relationships, including those with their children and spouse.[69] If large pieces of our children's development happen while they are young, by the time a person is fifty years old it is getting late to have the impact we want!

Our consumerist version of the American Dream comes at a high price for our children. Owning a nice home, taking great vacations, driving a new car, and buying every new electronic device on the market may help me keep up with the Jones family, but those purchases accomplish little for me when it comes to raising my children properly. God blessed me tremendously with my daughters. They are great kids, and my husband and I are very proud of them. There are days, however, that I wonder if it is more through God's grace than any parenting skill on my part. They are turning out fine in spite of my effort.

I believe that when it comes to our kids America may be getting what it pays for. And what we pay for is a new car every 4-5 years, an additional room in our homes, and TV sets and computers everywhere. No wonder we never see our children or converse with them. One of the most popular rooms added to the floor plans during the 1970's was a family room. It seemed as if building a family room meant it might be possible to be a family. But we began working more hours to pay for that room and all the cool new stuff we were accumulating at the expense of the family we hoped to be. A higher standard of living for the family turned into a lower quality of family life for many children.

While we might say we like kids, try to pass a school budget in your town. Test how your friends and neighbors really feel about investing in kids. Look at the salaries of pre-school teachers and professionals who make their living in careers that raise our children, as compared to careers in computer science or sales. Children do not come out at the top of the list.

So if God calls us to invest in our children, how are we doing? America's kids are more prone to depression, suicide and stress related illnesses than their parent's generation, and are less likely to call themselves happy. Their parents spend fewer hours and less quality time with them each day, and many now attend schools with larger classes and fewer teachers than a decade ago[70].

Children report being less happy than their parent's generation, despite the abundance of stuff with which they are showered[71]. I remember the iPod my daughter had to have. She kept uttering those memorable words, "all my friends have one." Though we did not rush right out and grab one, we took a family collection and bought it for her birthday. It was astonishing to see how quickly it did not matter. It never became the prized possession we expected, given how much she had wanted it.

I contrast this story to one my cousin shared. A career military man, he was stationed in Central America at the time. The poverty was overwhelming. Watching the kids play soccer with a ball that was mostly duct tape, he could not help but think of the piles of toys he knew his own daughter had back home. He and his friends bought some sports equipment and gave them to the youngsters who hung out near the barracks. He describes a response that was like nothing he had encountered before. They held the gifts with reverence. Months later, they were still carrying the equipment around like the crown jewels.

Our children, however, expect more and care for their stuff less. America's kids have gone from outdoor enthusiasts with friends on every street corner to overweight cave dwellers, leaving their rooms to forage for food in the family fridge or to make the semi-weekly jaunt to buy stuff at the mall.

My youngest can text an entire conversation on her cell phone before I have pecked out a few words. She is on track to be the first teenager to develop carpal tunnel without holding down a job. Homework for me meant sitting at the desk in my silent room. For her it involves a roaring TV, a computer screen with a window open for MySpace and FaceBook, and another to Google information for whatever assignments she has, and her cell phone to respond to any incoming tales of woe from friends. The TV has to be loud in order for her to hear it over her iPod.

I created this. I gave her a TV in her room, a computer to share with her sister, and an iPod that became obsolete in 8 months. Why should she leave her room for any one-on-one contact, when she can bring the entire world to her, all at the touch of a few key-strokes? I know that she is growing up in a world that teaches her to view her worth based on what her friends think of her. Unless I teach her another way, how can I ever expect her to see things through a different lens? When she was little, there were 20 Christmas presents under the tree with her name on them, and it is only now I am having second thoughts?

From their birth, our children are shoved onto a treadmill. Off to pre-school, play dates and Little League by six. Good schools, good grades and good jobs are all part of the social ladder held before them. *"Children feel stress long before they grow up. Many children have to cope with family conflict, divorce, constant changes in schools, neighborhoods and child care arrangements, peer pressure, and sometimes, even violence in their homes or communities.*[72]*"* They increasingly show signs of stress from the busy-ness of their lives[73]. No wonder they hide in their room when they get home from school. At least at home they can pull the world in around them. At least at home they hold some control over what gets to bombard them.

I think back to my own childhood with wonder. I lived in a small village until I was ten, and my best friend was only a few houses away. My brother and I rode bikes all day. No one came in the house at night until mothers stood on porches and started call-ing for their kids. It was kind of like a human version of the tele-graph. It did not really matter if it was your own Mom you heard or not—you just started home knowing somewhere down the street she was calling too.

Every now and then we would get a pickup game of baseball going, and everybody from town would grab a glove. Sometimes the mail carrier even walked down and joined us at the end of his day. The big kids played the most, but they usually worked the younger ones into the lineup too. When summer turned to winter, sleds replaced bats and balls. Most of us could be found on the town's one big hill soon after we got off the school bus at night.

Spending time in our room was considered a punishment. No one wanted to go in there because it meant being stuck inside all by yourself. I remember lying draped across my bed one evening, staring out the window at my friends running up and down the street below me. I had mouthed off to my Mom within Dad's hearing, the magic recipe for a time out in my room. I was despondent. I was stuck inside on a beautiful spring evening when everyone else was outside.

Now, twenty-five years later, I am trying to pry my kids out of their rooms. They are bombarded from the moment they wake up in the morning to the time they go to bed at night. TV shows and advertisements, telephone calls and text messages, MySpace and FaceBook, DVD's and video games. Do your chores, off to youth group, and back home for homework. Babysitting gigs and friends at the mall, soccer practice and piano lessons. Life never slows down, never takes a breather. And my girls are only young teens. No wonder they hole up. Their rooms are a refuge in a busy world they cannot get ahead of and do not fully understand.

If I was a mom thirty years ago, I would have been there more to level the playing field. Now I cannot identify the playing field, let alone help level it. I want my children to have the same experiences and enjoy the same kind of childhood I did, but the world I created for them makes it too easy to escape into their rooms and contact friends from afar.

I have to admit reality. I raised my children with privileges only one tenth of the world can afford and they assume that is just the way it is. Though they take mission trips with me and see the world's realities, they still come home to their friends in Aéropostale shirts, Nike shoes and laptop computers. They still plan to find ways to get all those things for themselves.

Like many youngsters in church in the 1960's, I was taught to tithe my allowance to the church. I got 75 cents, about the going rate among my peers at the time, and my Dad made me round up. That meant a dime went to church. I never questioned it. I just dropped it in the offering plate when it came around. It was never mine, and I never counted on it. That part of my allowance went to church. So ingrained was the habit, that when my grandmother gave each of us a thousand dollars at the time of my grandfather's death, I bought a tree for the front lawn of the church with $150 dollars of it.

My daughters receive twelve dollars a week. One dollar goes to church, and one goes to savings. I made my first mistake by letting them round down—their tithe should really be $1.20 cents. My bigger mistake, though, is not helping them see God in their giving. To them, it is just the $1.00 set aside each week. When enough tithes make it worth the effort they are stuffed in an offering envelop and brought to church. I have done a poor job to help them see that all they have is a blessing from God. I did not instill in them a desire to share in a consistent, systematic way so that through them God can care for others less fortunate (2 Corinthians 9).

Christ said *"let the children come to me,"* (Matthew 19:14) and Proverbs calls us to raise them in the way we want them to go so they will stick to it later in life (Proverbs 22:6). Using this biblical scorecard, my grade is a C- at best. I want them to care more for others than themselves, yet I am raising them in a nation where it is normal to buy them iPods, cell phones, five pair of jeans and twenty-three shirts when whole continents still struggle to provide the majority of their citizens with running water. I want my daughters to put the Lord first in their lives. At the same time I let soccer matches and overnights with friends creep into Sunday worship time and Wednesday night youth group. Without more of my time given to them how will I know if they are picking up the values that matter to me?

When it comes to my kids, swimming upstream is not going so well for me. While I know what I want to do and believe it is the right thing, when it comes to asking my already introverted children to be unconcerned about what they wear, I cannot seem to pull it off. I want my kids to do well and to feel good about who they are, but all too often I let the culture dictate what that looks like. I have this nagging feeling that if I do not get with it, I too will add to the number of spoiled, entitled children cast into the world. At least I have not yet made the biggest of all mistakes—believing that it is too late to make a difference.

I remember the time I was trying to rebuild the children's camps where I was employed. I keep doing this—taking a job at a camp just in time for their septic systems to fail dramatically, dozens of roofs to require replacement, new cabins needing to be built, bathrooms that must be installed and roadways paved. Moreover, I must do all this on a budget that has not seen the north side of balanced in years.

With a great deal of help we raised the money and got the projects underway. Hundreds of thousands went into septic systems, electrical work and water systems. New cabins were built. Existing buildings were remodeled to meet modern standards. Ten long years later, I could look back at what we had accomplished, and feel good about it all.

Here one of life's great ironies is revealed. My friend, a man with far more education and experience in the camping industry, shared that he had written my two camps off a decade ago. He did not see them turning around quickly enough to make it. I know if he had told me that up front I never would have tried turning them around. I had such respect for him and his opinions I too would have seen them as lost causes. Therein lays our hope of it not being too late with our children.

Our children and youth do not know that it is too late to make a difference in the consumer culture. They do not know it is too late for global warming to reverse, that water cannot be restored to empty lakes, that free time cannot be squeezed out of our busy lifestyles, and that there is nothing else to do with a Saturday afternoon besides buy stuff at the mall. They do not think change is impossible. What is more, and I smile as I write this given the principle of the adolescent who rebels against their parents, telling our youth it is too late will guarantee their success!

Our kids will change the world. Only if we begin teaching them in the way we want them to go, and finding ways for them to meet Christ regularly will they change it positively. They could lead a Romans 12 revolution; they could transform culture by centering their minds on God; they could carry the load. We must teach them how. If I want to make a difference in the world of tomorrow, it needs to happen at home with my kids today. Recycling trash, buying less stuff, wearing clothes longer, carpooling, using energy efficient light bulbs, are patterns that begin at home. Befriending and sharing our abundance with people who do not have the same access to resources as we are also important.

Our kids can change the world, if we teach them how. First, though, we need to show up for the job.

Questions for further reflection:
1. Have you bought any luxury gift for your children lately? Describe why you did and what their response was a month later.
2. Are you happy with the values your children hold dear?
3. With whom or what are your children spending time? Do you feel good about these role models?
4. Can you envision ways to become more influential in their lives, and to guide their thinking in directions that might go against the flow?

Action Plan:
- There is no substitute for getting involved in the life of your child. If you want to train them, start! Consider planning a night once a month where you focus on just one of your children. Take them for ice cream, go play tennis, or take a walk.
- Plan a family service trip. Organize one through church, or connect with an outside service organization. Few things have the same impact that first hand service does.
- Volunteer at the homeless shelter or soup kitchen.
- Choose an organization your family wants to focus on this Christmas. Ask for their wish list, and spend a significant portion of this year's Christmas budget helping them get something they need. Then volunteer with the organization as a family.
- Consider gifts of experience. Instead of the usual gift card or new shirt, do something that brings you together as a family.

If you want to know more:
- Read George Barna – *Transforming Children into Spiritual Champions; Revolutionary Parenting*
- Read Peggy Kendall, *Connected: Christian Parenting in an Age of IM and MySpace.*
- www.Safekids.com

Swimming Upstream

"Mama, why do we only give our leftovers to the homeless people?" My daughter asked me this question when she was nearly ready for kindergarten. It was a warm, spring night and we were driving away from a makeshift homeless camp by the freeway where we had, for the umpteenth time, dropped off the leftover pizza and pop from our congregation's midweek children's program.

I try to model my values for my children. I was so proud of the lesson I thought I was teaching my children by marching them down into this homeless camp, week after week, to deliver food. But that did not make sense to my young daughters. These people were sleeping on the ground, and the best we could do was a few pieces of cold pizza and half a bottle of pop? Innately, my girls knew we could do more.

In almost thirty years of working with children and parenting my own, I know one of the most important truths we can teach children is *get less, give more.* We must live our lives in ways that show our children Christ was serious when he told us the last will be first and whatever we do for the least of these we do for him (Matthew 25:40). We need to model this for our kids. We must show them how to do it.

I also try to encourage children to think through these issues on their own. Conversations around our own dinner tables about the number of people in our world who do not have enough to eat, bedtime prayers for folks who have no beds, regular volunteer shifts at our community's soup kitchen, donating old clothes and toys to a shelter, routine tithing and involving them in where they would like to give are easy, tangible, demonstrative ways of instilling a spirit of giving. Children are born with tender hearts and generous spirits. As people of faith who care about kids, we must be compelled to protect those hearts and nurture those spirits. The prophet Isaiah said that a little child would lead us (Isaiah 11:6). I realize Jesus knew what he was talking about when I recall my daughter's question about giving leftovers to homeless people.

Church – the new School in Town
The teaching and mentoring role of the church

We ought to change the legend on our money from "In God We Trust" to "In Money We Trust." Because, as a nation, we've got far more faith in money these days than we do in God.

Arthur Hoppe

Almost all plans fail, but you have to start with a plan.

General Patton

Hang in with me for just a bit longer with this swimming upstream idea. At the root of who I am I believe God answers all of life's questions. The problem is that many of us stop asking God for an opinion. As our culture further marginalizes God, those who claim to follow God look less and less like the people of God.

We live our lives as if they are a chest of drawers. The bottom drawer is full of our work clothes, and we pull them out for more than forty hours each week and live in them at work. The next drawer up in our metaphorical chest is for our clothes for home. We drag them out each night and on most weekends, as we putter around the house and spend time with our families. The top drawer is for church clothes. We put them on top because we know they are important, but we pull them out on a couple Sundays a month, at Christmas and Easter and when Mom visits.

These top-drawer clothes are important to us and we like them, but they do not integrate with the rest of our lives. Family is family, work is work, and God is God. The three rarely mix. Only in times of crisis, do we wonder what God has to say about our family. We rarely think about how God enters the picture at work.

We divided God among our life compartments. The Lord comes to our attention on Sundays as we seek to worship God and gives thanks for all we have been given. Little time is spent during the rest of the week reading scripture or prayerfully reflecting about what God says to us. The less time we spend with God in reflection and then acting upon what we discover, the less we look like the people with whom Christ builds his kingdom.

We must move God out of the top drawers of our lives and integrate the Lord into every drawer. After all, if we do not teach others what God says to us about our lifestyles, who do we think will? Our culture goes with the flow. We Christians try to swim upstream. It requires us, and our congregations, to be active in teaching how to swim upstream.

When I started writing my thoughts on consumerism and my stewardship of God's gifts, it was with a vague sense of unease, a feeling I was not doing quite what God had in mind. I had the feeling that God wanted me to give a tithe and I knew loving my neighbor was important. I did not give it a lot of thought, however. Years later, I recognize that God actually has a lot to say about all this, and God gave us the church to help us learn it.

I remember a story from my childhood. The pastor placed ten oranges on the table in front of us, and then used them as a way to explain what giving to the Lord meant. He told us that all these oranges were a gift from God. As followers of Christ we can say thank-you by giving back one tenth of what we had each Sunday (one orange). That meant if God gave us ten oranges, and we returned one as a thank you to God, our thank you would help God give an orange to someone else who needed one.

The story was a little literal for me. It was years before I grasped that this involved my money, not just my oranges! Eventually I got the hang of what tithing meant, though it would still be many more years before I tithed regularly.

Many of us never get beyond oranges when it comes to what God has to say about stewardship. In fact, many of us dislike the word stewardship. It is often equated with requests for money or boring sermons that tell us why we ought to give more money to God. Whole rows of people do not show up on the Sunday mornings if they know the stewardship word is going to be spoken.

This is a mistake. Substitute the word *care* for stewardship. God has a lot to say about how we care for things—our time, our lives, our families, even our relationships with friends and enemies. When we avoid God's word on the care taking of our lives, we leave ourselves open to a great deal of unnecessary missteps, pain and sorrow. The church is in the best position to help people learn what God has to say about how they should care for their lives, and it is critical the church take that responsibility seriously. Time is of the essence.

The planet is in peril, and the Lord has much to say about our responsibilities. Billions live in poverty, and God has given us instructions to share. People suffer from depression and anxiety, yet God laid out a plan for living life in a way that takes stress and loneliness away. Millions struggle with happiness and contentment. God teaches us to live a life of purpose. Too many children are raising themselves. God gives us a vision for the importance of family and friends and community so that children are not abandoned. Unless the church participates in this plan, lays out those directions for living, and teaches that message about creation care, it will not be taught. God's intentions form a counter-cultural message. The church is in possession of this message and is called to act upon it.

I will use the word *ought* now. The church *ought* to view one of its primary functions as teaching people what God has to say about stewardship—the care-taking of one's whole life. The church needs to teach it and model it in its own affairs. Such teaching passes along God's values on how we spend our time, accumulate possessions, care for our neighbors, prioritize our lives, care for creations and teach our children. The church lost its vision for teaching the counter-cultural message of stewardship. Our people are perishing in the alternate message of the culture. It is time to claim the real message again.

Not only are we failing to teach people how to swim upstream, few churches spend more than a sermon or two a year in helping people know it is good to try. As a result, people buy what does not make them happy with money they do not have; they work too many hours on things that are not important and spend too little time on what matters; they drive their bodies to the limit and fill them up with processed foods and too little sleep; and they consume the earth's resources as if there is a never ending supply. In the midst of it all, the church is silent.

It is time for the church to teach about swimming upstream. If we teach well, when Christians are surveyed, there would be a stark difference in their responses from the culture around them.

The picture of a Christian would be a life focused on people and not on the accumulation of stuff. Stories would be shared of coaching Little League, helping neighbors, and serving the world's poor. These stories would replace tales of the McMansions we purchased and the hours we work to make the payments, the divorces we added into our disposable lifestyle, and the money we dream of saving to make sure we have enough.

Americans are struggling with debt. We often saddle our future with huge home mortgages, car payments and credit card purchases. As the payments come due, the stress rises and the work hours increase. A church trying to teach God's word about management could enter this picture in a number of ways.

The church could begin or continue offering classes on financial management. Beginning with children in Sunday school, basic principles about the value of savings, the joy of giving, and the need to take care of the earth could be taught. Crown Financial Ministries or Dave Ramsey courses or Good Sense Ministry could become a part of the regular teaching ministry of the church. Perhaps a local and gifted financial counselor could provide a more tangible teaching presence. As people work through these courses and acquire tools to swim upstream, accountability could be formed with fellow travelers.

Those who demonstrate skill in good financial management could be tapped to mentor individuals who struggle. Relationships could be built with Christian financial planners and accountants outside the church. A community based program could start. This program could offering debt counseling and sound financial management to those not yet relating to a church community.

As the church serves within the community it will discover other arenas where need could be addressed. Debt, English as a second language, single parenting, substance recovery, divorce ministries, seniors in poverty – any number of ways can emerge for the local church to be the hands and feet of Christ in the neighborhoods outside their doors. No church has to do it all, but every church can do *something*.

Maybe you prefer to begin with creation care. A church convinced God had a different plan for our managing the earth might begin by choosing a stretch of highway nearby, and making it their responsibility to keep it clean. Young and old alike could volunteer two Saturdays a year to help walk the stretch and pick up the mess. The benefits could be enormous. Not only will the beauty of God's creation shine through, but children and youth will be mentored. Through the modeling of others, an appreciation for cleaning up our messes, being part of solving problems that others created, and learning to care for the commons (those areas that belong to everyone) will be nurtured in children and youth.

As churches undertake such projects, signs would spring up along the highways nationwide saying, "This stretch of highway is kept beautiful by (fill in the name of your church here)." Individuals and communities would begin to see the church as a major force in caring for creation.

As volunteers walk roadways, the bigger problem becomes far more visible. Plastic shopping bags, fast food wrappers and soda cans are exposed as the nuisances they are. Those educated in creation care would see the value of buying reusable cloth grocery bags and less plastic, and lobbying for more recycling programs and the use of less packaging. Once people actually get involved in cleaning up the mess, they also invest in making less of one! All this could result from churches focusing their people on becoming better caretakers of all that God has given them.

Romans chapter twelve calls for transformed hearts. It calls each of us to examine our culture and compare it to what we believe God asked us to create. When we make this comparison we become open to God's renewal of our thinking, and we can live a life much more in line with God's plan.

It is time for the church to begin an all out Romans 12 movement. It is time for the culture to shift. Our church clothes must come out of the top drawer and become our everyday wear. As people of Romans 12, our thinking will need to focus less on the stuff of this world—new cars and big screen HD televisions, bigger homes and the right clothes—and to focus on people. Such a shift will make us happier and healthier. It will bring heaven to millions more here on earth.

It is time for a Romans 12 movement, and I plan to play a part. If you care to join me, I could use some help in learning to swim upstream.

Action Plan
- Begin a Romans 12 movement in your church. Start small. Begin by having a small group ministry focus on this book or others like it, and then prayerfully consider where God calls your congregation.
- Ask your congregation's leaders to consider the role of stewardship education as part of the ministry. Encourage them to consider creating a year round education plan, and if possible, to assign staff and volunteers to implement it.
- Find one immediate step you personally can take to become a person of Romans 12. Implement it immediately.
- Sit down as a family, and discuss what it means to be people of Romans 12.

If you want to know more
- www.christineroush.net
- www.rjcrandallassociates.com
- www.DesignGroupInternational.com
- Ronald Vallet, *Stepping Stones of a Steward*
- George Barna, *How to Increase Giving in Your Church*
- Mark L. Vincent, *A Christian View of Money*

Swimming Upstream

First Baptist[74] started small. Issues of consumerism and stewardship had been popping up for years and were viewed as lack of good teaching about tithing. Over time it became obvious that failure to tithe was only part of the problem. The church had not discussed stewardship nor addressed the consumer culture in any meaningful way for twenty years. As financial problems rose in families and for the church, the church finally decided to take a closer look at stewardship education.

The church finance committee decided to start with a year round calendar. In November, a planning calendar was worked out so that consumerism and stewardship would be addressed in some fashion every month for the next twelve months. The pastor planned to preach a three part series on bible lessons on how God wants Christians to use their time. Children's messages were added to other months where a stewardship principle was explained in ways for the children to grasp God's word. A ten-week adult Christian education class was offered that focused on a biblical use of money. Individuals brought testimony about their experience with giving as part of the offertory.

The focus was never on why a person must give money to the church. Instead, it was a sharing of information about what Gods says is best to do with the blessings God gives. The church asked, "What do you hear God asking you to consider in terms of time, your resources and abilities over the next year?"

Epilogue
Reflections from a fellow swimmer

For twenty years, I have sought out what God says to me about how I manage everything entrusted to me. I wish I were further ahead. I paid attention early on because I knew the Bible had something to say about tithing. I heard pastors preach on it through the years, usually in the fall around church budget building time. Since I did not jump for joy at the prospect of giving away ten percent of my income, I chose guilt over giving. Though I had tithed from bigger windfalls since my teen years, I was not there yet with tithing as spiritual discipline.

I would like to have a story of a great spiritual awakening where I felt the Lord speaking directly to me, giving me a revelation that I needed to be more generous. Instead, I began serving on staff as a denominational camp director. Funding support was a regular subject as I began speaking in churches. I reached a point where it became an issue of my integrity. How could I tell all these great stories about kids reached for Christ, and ask for financial support, if I did not practice what the Bible invited me to do? This was hardly the greatest motivation for starting, but God seems to have been able to work with me anyway.

In my early years stewardship meant tithing. Tithing meant giving ten percent of what I had to the church. A lot has changed. I now prefer the word caretaking to stewardship because I believe God wants me to bring care to every area of life, not just money. What God cares about most is my focus as I live life. For instance, if I focus my life around money and possessions I will miss all the good stuff God has in store for me. This is why God wants to help me loosen the hold my stuff has on me. Some days I do a better job than other days. Other days, my stuff is still winning.

Developing these convictions has been slow. Early on, my husband and I had to find common ground between one spouse struggling with these issues, and one spouse not raised in a family that paid much attention to God. Those were hard conversations and compromises were tough to develop. My advice for those in similar circumstances? Keep at it. God honors the effort.

Eventually my understandings moved beyond money. I began to see how my time, my marriage, my friendships, and my compassion for those who had less also mattered. Ultimately, I came to believe that American culture has a terrible impact on my life, and that I enabled that culture to influence my children in the same bad ways. I decided to focus my academic studies on consumerism and stewardship. Fortunately for me, George Fox Seminary in Oregon made it possible to take a closer look at consumerism and culture, and this book is the result.

The more I discovered about consumerism and stewardship, the more I became convinced Romans 12 was written for this culture and for me. We moved so dramatically from the way God outlined for us, that the effects are found in every aspect of our lives. We are not content. Our stress levels are through the roof. We are blowing through limited natural resources at alarming rates. I learned that changing all this is an incredibly difficult thing to do.

Even with all I learned and my strong convictions that a Romans 12 movement is needed; even with my desire to live differently, I am still forced to work hard to arrive at any real change in my life. It feels as though all the forces of human nature and the culture that surround me are dead set against my making any change at all.

Despite these pressures, my family and I experienced some change and we feel good about it. One good example is in the vehicle we drive. We started our married life believing the car you drove said a lot about you. Consequently, we bought more car than we could afford.

The problem with buying too much car is that it loses a significant portion of its value before it even pulls into your driveway for the first time. This was compounded for us because I put 25,000 miles a year on the vehicle due to my work. Within three years we were driving a car with 100,000 miles on it, and with two years left on the loan. We rolled all that into a newer car and an even bigger loan, extending the pain well into the future. We finally said enough. We decided to drive the car into the ground and come out the other end with the car paid off.

We reached that goal, and drove the same Ford Taurus wagon four years beyond its last car payment. We have no current plans to sell it. Our goal is to save enough money to pay cash for the next vehicle, and buy one that is used. So far our savings mean that used vehicle is going to be old and have many miles, but we will have refused to let our car drive us into unnecessary debt.

Another area of success for us has been in bringing stuff home. All of us have seen progress here, especially one of my daughters. My youngest never met a dollar store she could not love. She would come home after any trip to a mall with a bag full of stuff she could not resist. Her room looked like a bomb went off in a garage sale. Helping her clean her room was a painful process as we were overwhelmed by the sheer magnitude of the piles of her stuff.

She finally reached a tipping point. She began to associate simplicity and order with a sense of peace. She divested the junk in her room and found a home for everything she kept. Her room is often the neatest in the house. The miracle of this transformation ranks up there with turning water into wine!

My husband and I have also become more careful about what we buy. We have come to enjoy rooms that are open and uncluttered and closets where you find what you seek. When something new moves into our house, we make sure something old or unused moves out, keep life more simple. We buy with a purpose, search for quality and make things last.

We also began bringing our daughters into more of our conversations, living out what Proverbs says about teaching a child the way you want them to live (Proverbs 22:6), so that when they are old they will remember it. Their participation led to discussions about switching to fluorescent lights, eating more local produce and making use of reusable cloth shopping bags at the grocery store. When we purchased our most recent clothes washer we bought the high efficiency front loader. While it cost more than a top loader, it was hard to make any other choice given what I have learned about the growing water crisis. In addition to these steps, wrestling with Romans 12 helped us discuss how we spent our holidays and how we might focus on something besides gift giving.

We still have a ways to go. Electronics trip us up on a regular basis. Though I believe strongly in buying well and using it for a long time, the sheer pace of technology conquers me. Despite my best intentions, my new laptop will be outdated in three years, the High Definition system for my movies and TV will have been replaced by some new technology and my cell phone will have become obsolete.

Speaking only for myself, I have yet to reduce stress significantly or to live at a more graceful pace. Everything still happens too quickly for me and I still try to take on far more than can be done. My jaw still hurts from clenching my teeth so much in my sleep. I still focus more effort on things I want, as opposed to things I need.

I am choosing to take my own advice and have picked an action item to engage from the end of most my chapters. Already, one of the most meaningful actions has been to spend time at the end of each day thanking God for all my blessings. Thanksgiving helped me build a sense of contentment as I realize how much I already have in my life.

I want to start a Romans 12 movement. I do not believe we as a nation are particularly happy with the way things are going in our world, and I believe some counter-cultural thinking is exactly what is required to turn that around. I believe God wants us to start swimming upstream. I am starting with me, and I invite you to join me. I am encouraging my church to form a Romans 12 team. If enough of us start, eventually we can become the current in the stream. Our world will be a better place for our efforts.

Visit www.christineroush.net for more information about this Romans 12 movement, and to become a participant in the ongoing conversation.

Endnotes

1 Robert H. Frank, "Our Climb to Sublime, Hold On. We Don't Need to Go There," *Washington Post*01/24/99.

2 David G. Myers, *The American Paradox*(New Haven: Yale University Press, 2000). 126-160.

3 Ibid, 137.

4 *Dear friends, God is good. So I beg you to offer your bodies to him as a living sacrifice, pure and pleasing. That is the most sensible way to serve God. 2Don't be like the people of this world, but let God change the way you think. Then you will know how to do everything that is good and pleasing to him.* (Romans 12:1,2 CEV)

5 Ronald J. Sider, *Rich Christians in an Age of Hunger: Moving from Affluence to Generosity,* 20th anniversary revision ed. (Dallas: Word Publishing 1997), 2.

6 "Faith Has Limited Effect on Most People's Behavior," 5-24-04, <http://www.barna.org/FlexPage.aspx?Page=BarnaUpdate& BarnaUpdateID=164>

7 Larry Burkett, and Rick Osborne, *Financial Parenting*(Chicago: Moody Press, 1996), 12.

8 "USA Today Snapshot", Gannett Company www.usatoday.com/snapshot/money/snapindex.htm. (accessed 12/02 2005).

9 Ronald J. Sider, *Rich Christians in an Age of Hunger: Moving from Affluence to Generosity*, 20th anniversary revision. ed.(Dallas: Word Publishing, 1997), 9.

10 Juliet Schor, *The Overworked American: The Unexpected Decline of Leisure*(New York: Basic Books, 1992), 111.

11 http://www.americangaming.org/Industry/factsheets/ statistics_detail.cfv?id=7.

12 "Snapshot," *USA Today*, May 15 1996.

13 "Snapshot".

14 Chris Isidore, "The Zero Savings Problem," (03 August 2005). http://money.cnn.com/2005/08/02/news/economy/savings/ind ex.htm (accessed 26 March 2006).

[15] I am not happy with my bathroom scales on Monday mornings or that my daughter is now an inch taller than I am either, but that is beside the point.

[16] Paco Underhill, *Why We Buy: The Science of Shopping* (Simon & Schuster, 2000).

[17] Rodney Clapp, "Why the Devil Takes Visa," *Christianity Today*, 07 October 1996.

[18] Ibid.

[19] James B. Simpson, Bartleby.com http://www.bartleby.com/63/16/2216.html (accessed December 7 2005).

[20] Erica Wintraub Austin, Ph.D.; et.al., "Benefits and Costs of Channel One in a Middle School Setting and the Role of Media-Literacy Training." (*Pediatrics* 117, no.3 (2006).

[21] http://www.santarosa.fl.gov/extension/documents/articles/fce1002.pdf.

[22] Torstein Veblen, *Theory of the Leisure Class,* Penguin Classics, 1994.

[23] Thomas Stanley and William Danko, *The Millionaire Next Door,* New York: Pocket Books, 1996.

[24] Dave Ramsey, *Financial Peace* (New York: Viking, 1992), 8.

[25] Jessica Bennett, August 8 (2006, accessed December 6 2006); available from www.msnbc.msn.com/id/14251360/site/newsweek/.

[26] Bill McKibben, *The End of Nature*(New York: Random House, 2006), xxiii.

[27] Lester Brown, *Plan B 2.0: Rescuing a Planet under Stress and a Civilization in Trouble*(New York: W.W. Norton and Company, 2006), 4-5.

[28] Myers, 186.

[29] Fred Pearce, *When the Rivers Run Dry.* Boston: Beacon Press, 2006.

[30] Lester Brown, *Plan B 2.0* . . . .

[31] http://www.worldwatch.org/node/1499

[32] Craig Blomberg, *Neither Poverty nor Riches: A Biblical Theology of Material Possessions*(Grand Rapids: Eerdmans, 1999), 8.

[33] Schor, 11.

34 Ibid.

35 Myers, 137-8.

36 Ibid.

37 Proverbs 22:6

38 Myers, 235.

39 David G. Myers, "Pursuing Happiness," *Psychology Today*, July/August 1993.

40 Matthew 22:34-40

41 .Mark L. Vincent, *A Christian View of Money (3rd ed.)* Eugene, OR, Wipf and Stock. 2007.s

42 "The Potential," *Empty Tomb* (2007). www.emptytomb.org (accessed 10/31).

43 Giving USA. *Giving USA 2006: The Annual Report on Philan-thropy for the Year 2005*. Indianapolis: Indiana University— Purdue University Indianapolis.

44 Juliet Schor, *The Overspent American: Why We Want What We Don't Need*(New York, New York: HarperPerennial, 1998), 113.

45 Ibid, 6.

46 Sider, 39.

47 , www.emptytomb.org.

48 Luke 6:41,42

49 Brian Tracy, *Eat That Frog!*(Hodder & Stoughton 2004), 3.

50 Schor, *The Overspent American: Why We Want What We Don't Need*, 89.

51 Juliet Schor, *The Overworked American: The Unexpected Decline of Leisure* (New York: Basic Books, 1992), 22.

52 Schor, *The Overworked American: The Unexpected Decline of Leisure*, 22.

53 "Consumers Eager for Spring as Easter Spending Increases," *National Retail Federation*, no. March 20, 2007 (2007). http://www.nrf.com/modules.php?name=News&op=viewlive &sp_id=235 (accessed 10/08).

54 http://articles.moneycentral.msn.com/Investing/ StockInvestingTrading/retailers-face-not-so-happy-holidays.aspx#pageTopAnchor.

55 Kim Murphy, "Polluted Willamette River Sullies Image of a Green Oregon," *LA Times*, April 8, 2000.

56 http://www.vatican.va/holy_father/john_paul_ii/messages/ peace/docuemtns/hf_jp-ii_mes_19891208_xxIII-world-day-for-peace_en.html.

57 Thomas Peters and Robert H. Waterman, Jr. *In Search of Excellence: Lessons from America's Best-Run Companies.* New York: Harper Collins, 2004, pp.69-70.

58 David Bach. *The Automatic Millionaire: A Powerful One-Step Plan to Live and Finish Rich.* New York: Broadway Books, 2006.

59 David Myers. *The American Paradox: Spiritual Hunger in an Age of Plenty.* New Haven: Yale Press, 2000, 133.

60 Frank.

61 Gerald R. Gill, *The Meanness Mania.* Howard University Press, 1980.

62 Schor, *The Overspent American: Why We Want What We Don't Need*, 21.

63 Ibid., 18.

64 Ibid, 113.

65 Schor, *The Overspent American: Why We Want What We Don't Need*, 57.

66 Marlys Harris, "Forever Young," *Money*, October 2007.

67 http://money.cnn.com/2008/05/23/pf/credit_debt/index. htm?postversion=2008052713

68 Robert Fulghum, *All I Really Need to Know I Learned in Kindergarten: Uncommon Thoughts on Common Things.* New York: Villard Books, 1988.

69 Marlys Harris. *Forever Young.* Money Magazine, October 2007, pp.85-88

70 David G. Myers, *The American Paradox: Spiritual hunger in an age of plenty.* New Haven: Yale Press, 2000, 60-97.

71 Ibid.

72 http://www.aboutourkids.org/articles/stress_in_children_ what_it_how_parents_can_help.

73 http://www.time.com/time/magazine/article/ 0,9171,998857,00.html. See also, http://www. challengesuccess.org/.

74 This story is a composite case study of several congregations. "First Baptist" does not designate a specific congregation.